English Reading and Spelling
For the Spanish Speaker

Book 2

For Ages 10 - Adult

Written by
Kathleen Fisher

Illustrated by
Tracee Schmidt

Fisher Hill   Huntington Beach   California

Published by FISHER HILL
5267 Warner Avenue, #166
Huntington Beach, CA 92649-4079

Made in the U.S.A.

Publisher's Cataloging in Publication

Fisher, Kathleen S., 1952-
    English reading and spelling for the Spanish speaker. Book
2 / by Kathleen Fisher. --1st ed.
        p. cm.
        Audience: Ages 10-adult.
        Includes bibliographical references and index.
            ISBN 978-1-878253-25-5

            1. English language--Textbooks for foreign speakers--
Spanish. 2. English as a second language.

Table of Contents

Contenido

Introduction

The purpose of this book is to help Spanish speakers learn to read and spell English. Book 2 builds upon the speech sounds, vocabulary, spelling, and comprehension skills developed in Book 1. As in Book 1, Book 2 uses a systematic approach to teach the English speech sounds for reading and spelling. Book 2 continues to provide practice with phonemic awareness, which is the ability to identify individual sounds and their order within words. Learning the different speech sounds will help students read and spell English fluently. Eighty-five percent (85%) of words in English are phonetic. This book will also present many of the small commonly used words, called sight words, that are not phonetic.

This book is bilingual since the word list for each lesson is presented in English and Spanish. There are pictures to go with many of the words in the lists. Each lesson emphasizes one or two new speech sounds. The vowel sounds in English are different than those in Spanish, but many of the English consonant sounds are similar to those in Spanish. There are 26 letters in the English alphabet:

Upper Case
A B C D E F G H I J K L M N O P Q R S T U V W X Y Z

Lower Case
a b c d e f g h i j k l m n o p q r s t u v w x y z

The five vowel letters are a, e, i, o, u. All the other letters are consonants. Consonants have one sound except, for c and g, which have two sounds. Vowels can make several speech sounds. Sometimes the letter "y" is used as a vowel.

Words are made up of syllables (units of pronunciation). Some words have one syllable, while others have two or more syllables. Every syllable must have a vowel. If a word has three syllables then it has three vowel sounds.

Each lesson's word list begins with words that contain the speech sound that is being emphasized in that lesson. The last word or words in the list are sight words or homophones.

Practicing English speech sounds, sight words, and their spellings will help the Spanish speaker learn English reading and spelling.

Introducción

La finalidad de este libro es ayudar a las personas de habla hispana a leer y escribir en inglés. El Libro 2 expande sobre los sonidos del lenguaje hablado, el vocabulario y la comprensión desarrollada en el Libro 1. Como en el Libro 1, el Libro 2 usa un planteamiento sistemático de la enseñanza de los sonidos del inglés al leerlo y al deletrearlo. El Libro 2 continúa proporcionando práctica en la conciencia fonética, la cual es la facultad de identificar sonidos individuales y el orden que ocupan dentro de las palabras. Aprender los distintos sonidos del habla ayudará al estudiante a conocer la ortografía y a leer el inglés con fluidez. El ochenta y cinco por ciento (85%) de las palabras en inglés son fonéticas. Este libro también presentará muchas de las palabras pequeñas populares llamadas vocabulario visual que no son fonéticas.

Este libro es bilingüe porque en cada lección se presenta una lista de palabras en inglés y en español. Hay dibujos que acompañan a muchas de las palabras de las listas. Cada lección subraya uno o dos sonidos nuevos. Los sonidos de las vocales en inglés son diferentes a los de las vocales en español pero muchos de los sonidos de las consonantes en inglés son similares a los de las consonantes en español. Existen 26 letras en el alfabeto en inglés:

Mayúsculas
A B C D E F G H I J K L M N O P Q R S T U V W X Y Z

Minúsculas
a b c d e f g h i j k l m n o p q r s t u v w x y z

Las cinco letras vocales son a, e, i, o, u. Todas las demás letras son consonantes. Las consonantes tienen un sonido excepto la c y la g, éstas tienen dos sonidos. Las vocales pueden tener varios sonidos en el lenguaje hablado. En ocasiones la letra "y" se usa como vocal.

Las palabras se componen de sílabas (unidades de pronunciación). Algunas palabras son de una sílaba, otras tienen dos o más. Cada sílaba debe tener una vocal. Si una palabra tiene tres sílabas, entonces tendrá tres sonidos vocales.

Cada lista de palabras de las lecciones comienza con palabras que contienen el sonido hablado que se está explicando en la lección. La última palabra o palabras de la lista son del vocabulario visual u homófonos.

Practicar los sonidos hablados en inglés, el vocabulario visual y su ortografía le ayudará a la persona de habla hispana a aprender a leer y escribir correctamente el inglés.

Lesson 1 * Lección 1
Word List * La lista de las palabras

Cuando aparece la letra y̱ al final de una palabra corta, tiene el sonido de una /i/ larga, como suena en *by*.

Inglés	Español
1. by	junto a
2. my	mi
3. shy	tímido
4. dry	seco
5. cry	llorar
6. fry	freír
7. spy	espiar
8. fly	mosca
9. sly	astuto
10. grin	sonrisa
11. drip	goteo
12. track	pista
13. crack	quebradura
14. want	querer
15. do	verbo auxiliar

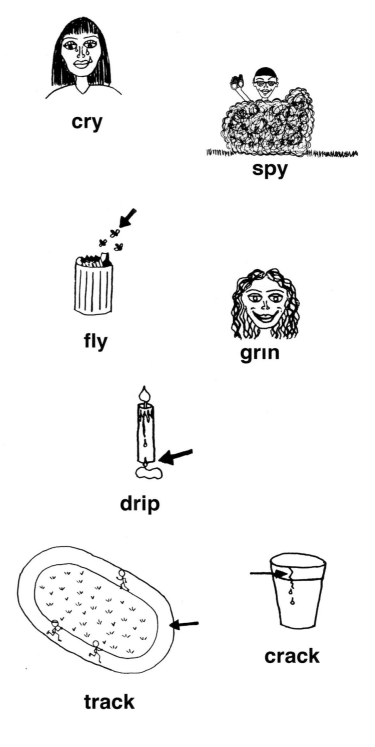

cry

spy

fly

grin

drip

track

crack

Sentences * Oraciones

Lea las oraciones. Después escriba el número de la oración debajo del dibujo correcto.

1. Do not step on the crack.

2. The spy grins at the deer.

3. Dad wants to fry the fish.

4. The sly fox tricks the duck.

5. The fly is stuck in a drop of mud.

6. The shy boy is by the big brass drum.

7. Meg sweeps the dry brush into the box.

8. My friend wants to cry.

9. The water will drip on the grass.

10. Do not play on the tracks.

Dibujos

a. _____

b. _____

c. _____

d. _____

e. _____

f. _____

g. _____

h. _____

i. _____

j. _____

Spelling Dictation * Dictado

Pídale a alguien que le dicte las palabras de la página 6. Después de escribirlas, LÉALAS y revise la ortografía. Corrija las palabras que estén equivocadas.

Fill in the Blanks * Llene el Espacio

Llene cada espacio con una palabra de la lista de palabras. Use cada palabra solamente una vez. Algunas oraciones tienen dibujos al final para ayudarle.

1. The slim man has a big _____.

2. The _____ dog flees from the big cat.

3. Do not _____ water on the rug.

4. _____ the red dress in the sun.

5. The pill fell in the _____ .

6. They _____ to play with the drum.

7. There is a big black _____ on the ham.

8. The _____ cat plays a trick on the rat.

9. Pat will _____ the clams in the pan.

10. The man will meet the _____ at the shack.

11. The green cup is _____ the black dish.

12. Do not slip on the _____ .

13. Where is _____ dog?

14. _____ not put the trash in the shed.

15. The doll can _____ and kiss.

Spelling Rules * Reglas de ortografía

Cuando se añade una s a las palabras que terminan en y, necesitará quitar la y y añadir ies excepto cuando una vocal preceda a la y, como en boy/boys. Use las palabras a la derecha para llenar los espacios en blanco. Quite la y y añada ies cuando sea necesario.

1. Pat _____ the big brass drum.

2. There are _____ on the beef.

3. Bill _____ the dishes with a rag.

4. They can fix the _____ .

5. Dan _____ the eggs in the hot pan.

6. Mom _____ a new black dress.

7. Tom _____ in the mud.

8. The _____ meet at the black van.

9. The boy _____ for his truck.

10. The green _____ swim in the water.

dry
want
fry
cry
slip
hear
fly
spy
frog
clock

4

WordSearch * Busca Palabras

Encuentra las palabras de la Lección 1 en el busca palabras. Marca las respuestas. Las palabras pueden estar escritas en forma normal, al revés o diagonalmente.

			shy
dry	fry	by	sly
do	want	my	

C	G	C	M	Y	S	Y	D
S	R	R	R	L	B	R	O
S	H	Y	I	A	Y	E	M
P	K	Y	F	N	C	T	B
Y	H	R	W	P	R	K	Y
Y	Y	A	I	A	F	K	L
V	N	R	C	I	G	L	S
T	D	K	L	V	O	D	Y

Answer Key * Las Respuestas

Sentences * Oraciones (page 2)

a. 7
b. 2
c. 6
d. 9
e. 4

f. 10
g. 5
h. 1
i. 8
j. 3

Spelling Dictation * Dictado (page 2)

grin, cross, shy, green, pass, said, stuck, drug, shop, pray, grass, crib, my, day, cliff; Do not drop the egg. The dog swam in the bay.

Fill in the Blanks * Llene el Espacio (page 3)

1. grin
2. shy
3. drip
4. Dry
5. crack
6. want
7. fly
8. sly

9. fry
10. spy
11. by
12. track
13. my
14. Do
15. cry

Spelling Rules * Reglas de ortografía (page 4)

1. hears	6. wants
2. flies	7. slips
3. dries	8. spies
4. clock	9. cries
5. fries	10. frogs

WordSearch * Busca Palabras (page 5)

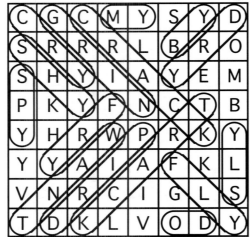

Lesson 2 * Lección 2

Word List * La lista de las palabras

La letra <u>e</u> o la letra <u>o</u> al final de las palabras cortas por lo general sonarán como vocales largas. Las excepciones son <u>to</u> y <u>do</u>.

Inglés	Español
1. me	me/mí
2. he	él
3. we	nosotros
4. she	ella
5. be	ser
6. no	no
7. go	ir
8. so	así
9. steep	empinado
10. trap	trampa
11. floss	hilo dental
12. stack	pila
13. give	dar
14. live	vivir
15. have to	tener que

he

we

she

no

floss

trap

7

Sentences * Oraciones

Lea las oraciones. Después escriba el número de la oración debajo del dibujo correcto.

1. Stack the boxes on the mat.

2. She will give the fish to the cat.

3. The ducks live in the shack.

4. I will be on the hill with the dog.

5. Do you have to fix the van?

6. Is the fox in the trap?

7. He flosses at the shed.

8. Do we have to go up the steep hill?

9. "No, do not give it to me," said Meg.

10. My friends and I will go to the bus stop.

Dibujos

a. _____

b. _____

c. _____

d. _____

e. _____

f. _____

g. _____

h. _____

i. _____

j. _____

Spelling Dictation * Dictado

Pídale a alguien que le dicte las palabras de la página 12. Después de escribirlas, LÉALAS y revise la ortografía. Corrija las palabras que estén equivocadas.

Fill in the Blanks * Llene el Espacio

Llene cada espacio con una palabra de la lista de palabras. Use cada palabra solamente una vez. Algunas oraciones tienen dibujos al final para ayudarle.

1. I hear a dog in the _____ .

2. _____ , where is your red dress?

3. _____ plans to quit his job.

4. They _____ on the hill in a big shack.

5. Do not grab _____ by the leg.

6. I _____ feed the pigs.

7. Here is the _____ of faxes.

8. _____ will meet the queen at the club.

9. He will _____ his mom a kiss.

10. _____ sat on the log with her friend.

11. We will _____ to the bay with the dogs.

12. If you bleed, do not _____ .

13. Will you _____ here by ten?

14. _____ , I will be there by four.

15. The hill is too _____ for the red van.

9

Spelling Rules * Reglas de ortografía

La letra <u>v</u> nunca se usa al final de una palabra. En las palabras que terminan con un sonido de <u>v</u>, tales como *have, give* y *live,* el marcador <u>e</u> se coloca al final de la palabra para no infringir la regla de la "v". El sonido de la vocal puede ser largo o corto.

have	give	live	love

Use las palabras anteriores en las oraciones a continuación. Use cada palabra una sola vez.

1. I _____ to feed the sheep on the hill.

2. We _____ to play with the dogs and cats.

3. The big black dogs _____ at the shack.

4. Mom will _____ the red sled to the boys.

Rhyming Words * Palabras que riman

Las palabras que riman son palabras que comienzan de manera diferente pero terminan con la misma vocal y los mismos sonidos en la terminación. Por ejemplo, *red, bed* y *said* son palabras que riman. No necesitan escribirse igual, pero necesitan terminar con la misma vocal y los mismos sonidos en la terminación. Use las palabras a la derecha para asociarlas con las palabras que rimen.

5. dress _____ day

6. buzz _____ stuck

7. bay _____ sun

8. two _____ black

9. sheet _____ press

10. quack _____ fuzz

11. truck _____ do

12. one _____ feet

WordSearch * Busca Palabras

Encuentra las palabras de la Lección 3 en el busca palabras. Marca las respuestas. Las palabras pueden estar escritas en forma normal, al revés o diagonalmente.

chill	**cheer**	**chat**	**much**
speech	**does**	**goes**	

s	c	h	i	l	l	f	q	o
m	p	v	u	k	h	h	f	h
u	z	e	c	f	c	c	t	n
c	l	e	e	k	i	n	a	i
h	h	p	o	c	r	u	h	h
c	c	h	i	p	h	l	c	c
c	h	o	p	r	e	e	h	c
d	o	e	s	s	s	e	h	c
c	h	i	c	k	g	o	e	s

Answer Key * Las Respuestas

Sentences * Oraciones (page 14)

a.	4	f.	2	
b.	1	g.	7	
c.	3	h.	9	
d.	10	i.	5	
e.	8	j.	6	

Spelling Dictation * Dictado (page 14)

so, crash, spy, check, she, bleed, drip, slim, chin, slick, cry, who, no, trap, way; Did you fry the fish for lunch? She will run to the red shed.

Fill in the Blanks * Llene el Espacio (page 15)

1.	lunch	9.	chick
2.	Does	10.	cheer
3.	chin	11.	chip
4.	speech	12.	chill
5.	chop	13.	check
6.	goes	14.	much
7.	rich	15.	chess
8.	chat		

Spelling Demons & Rhyming Words * Demonios de la ortografía y Palabras que riman (page16)

1.	Their	8.	to
2.	friend	9.	No
3.	too	10.	Yes
4.	There	11.	No
5.	Where	12.	Yes
6.	want	13.	Yes
7.	were		

WordSearch * Busca Palabras (page 17)

Lesson 3 * Lección 3

Word List * La lista de las palabras

Combine los sonidos de la consonante y la vocal para leer y entender la ortografía de las palabras. Las letras <u>ch</u> se pronuncian /ch/ como en *chip*.

Inglés	Español
1. chick	pollito
2. chip	"chip" de papa o tortilla
3. chop	cortar
4. chin	barbilla
5. check	cheque
6. chill	enfriar
7. cheer	animar
8. chat	charlar
9. chess	ajedrez
10. much	mucho
11. rich	rico
12. speech	discurso
13. lunch	almuerzo
14. does	verbo auxiliar
15. goes	va

chick

chip

chin

check

chess

rich

lunch

Sentences * Oraciones

Lea las oraciones. Después escriba el número de la oración debajo del dibujo correcto.

1. Your lunch is in the bag.

2. There is too much fuzz on my dress.

3. Do not drop the chip on the rug.

4. She goes to the shop with her mom.

5. I am glad to give the speech.

6. The chick is in the grass with the duck.

7. Meg can chop the tree.

8. There is a bug on your chin.

9. Pam plays chess with her friend.

10. He is a rich man.

Dibujos

a. _____

b. _____

c. _____

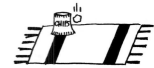
e. _____

f. _____

d. _____

g. _____

h. _____

i. _____

j. _____

Spelling Dictation * Dictado

Pídale a alguien que le dicte las palabras de la página 18. Después de escribirlas, LÉALAS y revise la ortografía. Corrija las palabras que estén equivocadas.

14

Fill in the Blanks * Llene el Espacio

Llene cada espacio con una palabra de la lista de palabras. Use cada palabra solamente una vez. Algunas oraciones tienen dibujos al final para ayudarle.

1. My friend and I have _____ at the club.

2. _____ the big bell go in the shed?

3. There is a cut on your _____ .

4. She will give a _____ at lunch.

5. Do not _____ up the log.

6. She _____ to the shed with four dogs.

7. The _____ man gives cash to the queen.

8. At lunch she will _____ with her friend.

9. Does the _____ sleep in the hay?

10. Bob will _____ for Pam.

11. Do not feed the _____ to the dog.

12. Sam will _____ the water for lunch.

13. Here is the _____ for the van.

14. You have too _____ cash for the dress.

15. They are glad to play _____ .

Spelling Demons * Demonios de la ortografía

Las siguientes palabras que se usan con frecuencia a menudo se escriben con mala ortografía.

their	there	were	where
to	too	want	friend

Use las palabras anteriores en las oraciones a continuación. Use cada palabra una sola vez.

1. _____ mom is sick in bed.

2. My _____ slips in the mud.

3. He plays _____ much chess.

4. _____ is a crack in the black dish.

5. _____ do I put the stack of checks?

6. They _____ to fry the fish.

7. Where _____ you at ten?

8. They want _____ give you a black pup.

Rhyming Words * Palabras que riman

Las palabras que riman son palabras que comienzan de manera diferente pero terminan con la misma vocal y los mismos sonidos en la terminación. Por ejemplo, *red, bed* y *said* son palabras que riman. No necesitan escribirse igual, pero necesitan terminar con la misma vocal y los mismos sonidos en la terminación.

Si las dos palabras riman, escriba "yes" (sí); si no, escriba "no" (no).

fish	kiss	9. _____
shy	fry	10. _____
goes	does	11. _____
chess	bless	12. _____
does	fuzz	13. _____

WordSearch * Busca Palabras

Encuentra las palabras de la Lección 3 en el busca palabras. Marca las respuestas. Las palabras pueden estar escritas en forma normal, al revés o diagonalmente.

chill	**cheer**	**chat**	**much**
speech	**does**	**goes**	

s	c	h	i	l	l	f	q	o
m	p	v	u	k	h	h	f	h
u	z	e	c	f	c	c	t	n
c	l	e	e	k	i	n	a	i
h	h	p	o	c	r	u	h	h
c	c	h	i	p	h	l	c	c
c	h	o	p	r	e	e	h	c
d	o	e	s	s	s	e	h	c
c	h	i	c	k	g	o	e	s

Answer Key * Las Respuestas

Sentences * Oraciones (page 14)

a. 4

b. 1

c. 3

d. 10

e. 8

f. 2

g. 7

h. 9

i. 5

j. 6

Spelling Dictation * Dictado (page 14)

so, crash, spy, check, she, bleed, drip, slim, chin, slick, cry, who, no, trap, way; Did you fry the fish for lunch? She will run to the red shed.

Fill in the Blanks * Llene el Espacio (page 15)

1. lunch

2. Does

3. chin

4. speech

5. chop

6. goes

7. rich

8. chat

9. chick

10. cheer

11. chip

12. chill

13. check

14. much

15. chess

Spelling Demons & Rhyming Words * Demonios de la ortografía y Palabras que riman (page16)

1.	Their	8.	to
2.	friend	9.	No
3.	too	10.	Yes
4.	There	11.	No
5.	Where	12.	Yes
6.	want	13.	Yes
7.	were		

WordSearch * Busca Palabras (page 17)

Lesson 4 * Lección 4

Word List * La lista de las palabras

Combine los sonidos de la consonante y la vocal para leer y entender la ortografía de las palabras. Las letras <u>or</u> se pronuncian /or/ como en *corn*.

Inglés	Español
1. corn	maíz
2. horn	corneta
3. sport	deporte
4. short	bajo
5. fort	fuerte
6. born	nacer
7. sort	separar
8. for	por/para
9. cord	cordón
10. fork	tenedor
11. storm	tormenta
12. torn	roto
13. pork	cerdo
14. please	por favor
15. says	dice

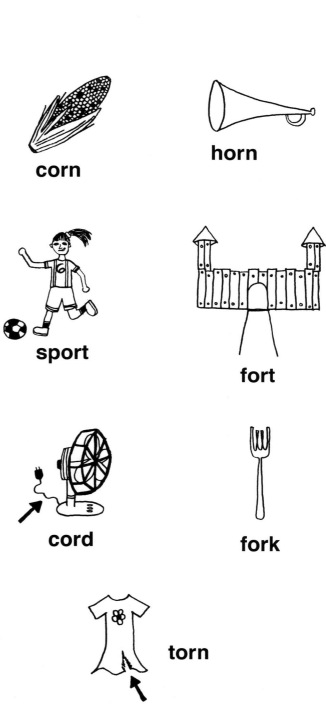

corn

horn

sport

fort

cord

fork

torn

Sentences * Oraciones

Lea las oraciones. Después escriba el número de la oración debajo del dibujo correcto.

1. Please do not grab my fork.

2. We will have corn and pork for lunch.

3. Six pups were born in the shed.

4. Your red dress is torn.

5. We will cheer with the horn and bell.

6. Please plug in the cord.

7. Pam and Bob will sort the cash.

8. She will pay for the gum.

9. The two short men are at the fort.

10. She plays the sport in the storm.

Dibujos

a.
_____

b.
_____

c.
_____

d.
_____

e.
_____

f.
_____

g.
_____

h.
_____

i.
_____

j.
_____

Spelling Dictation * Dictado

Pídale a alguien que le dicte las palabras de la página 24. Después de escribirlas, LÉALAS y revise la ortografía. Corrija las palabras que estén equivocadas.

Fill in the Blanks * Llene el Espacio

Llene cada espacio con una palabra de la lista de palabras. Use cada palabra solamente una vez. Algunas oraciones tienen dibujos al final para ayudarle.

1. He fed _____ to the pigs.

2. _____ give water to the cats.

3. Dad was _____ on May 9, 1962.

4. He plays his _____ at the bay.

5. _____ comes from pigs.

6. Where do I plug in the _____?

7. We do not put up the flag in the _____ .

8. The class will see the _____ on their trip.

9. They will _____ the red and black glasses.

10. I can hear the van's _____ .

11. The doll with the green dress is _____ Meg.

12. Please put the _____ next to the dish.

13. He _____ he fed the dogs.

14. The gray sheets were _____ in the storm.

15. The four _____ kids sit on the sled.

Verb Practice * Práctica con los verbos

Use los siguientes verbos en las oraciones a continuación. Use cada verbo una vez.

have	has	is	are
say	says	have to	gives

1. He _____ the red rock is in the box.

2. We _____ at the club with the queen.

3. We _____ a big shed in the back.

4. She _____ the red cap to her dad.

5. I _____ cut the grass.

6. The sly fox _____ in the shed with the chicks.

7. What will you _____?

8. She _____ a green bug on her neck.

Rhyming Words * Palabras que riman

Las palabras que riman son palabras que comienzan de manera diferente pero terminan con la misma vocal y los mismos sonidos en la terminación. Por ejemplo, *red, bed* y *said* son palabras que riman. No necesitan escribirse igual, pero necesitan terminar con la misma vocal y los mismos sonidos en la terminación. Use las palabras a la derecha para asociarlas con las palabras que rimen.

9. fork _____ sees

10. she _____ fort

11. sport _____ hop

12. please _____ pork

13. chop _____ had

14. glad _____ flee

WordSearch * Busca Palabras

Encuentra las palabras de la Lección 4 en el busca palabras. Marca las respuestas. Las palabras pueden estar escritas en forma normal, al revés o diagonalmente.

		short	born
sort	for	storm	pork
please	says		

e	h	o	r	n	c	f	c	b
s	s	o	a	j	o	t	o	f
p	l	a	r	r	r	r	s	o
o	k	t	e	o	n	b	o	r
r	r	o	h	l	d	h	r	t
t	o	s	n	k	p	r	t	f
v	p	r	f	h	r	p	o	o
a	o	s	y	a	s	o	m	c
c	s	t	o	r	m	e	f	d

Answer Key * Las Respuestas

Sentences * Oraciones (page 20)

a.	4	f.	2
b.	8	g.	6
c.	5	h.	7
d.	1	i.	3
e.	9	j.	10

Spelling Dictation * Dictado (page 20)

chop, he, are, horn, play, chat, fort, mash, fry, chill, we, was, tree, short, speed; Who was in the shed? The duck can not fly yet.

Fill in the Blanks * Llene el Espacio (page 21)

1.	corn	9.	sort
2.	Please	10.	horn
3.	born	11.	for
4.	sport	12.	fork
5.	Pork	13.	says
6.	cord	14.	torn
7.	storm	15.	short
8.	fort		

Verb Practice & Rhyming Words * Práctica con los verbos y Palabras que riman (page 22)

1.	says	8.	has
2.	are	9.	pork
3.	have	10.	flee
4.	gives	11.	fort
5.	have to	12.	sees
6.	is	13.	hop
7.	say	14.	had

WordSearch * Busca Palabras (page 23)

24

Lesson 5 * Lección 5

Word List * La lista de las palabras

Combine los sonidos de las letras para leer y entender la ortografía de las palabras. Las letras **all** se pronuncian /all/ como en *ball*.

Inglés	Español
1. ball	pelota
2. fall	caer
3. call	llamar
4. tall	alto
5. hall	pasillo
6. wall	muro
7. small	pequeño
8. mall	centro comercial
9. stall	puesto
10. drill	taladro
11. well	pozo
12. brass	latón
13. should	debería
14. would	verbo auxiliar
15. could	podría

ball

fall

call

wall

mall

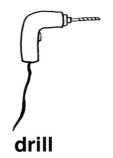

drill

well

Sentences * Oraciones

Lea las oraciones. Después escriba el número de la oración debajo del dibujo correcto.

1. There is water in the well.

2. The tall man is in the hall.

3. The drill has a torn cord.

4. Do not fall in the mud.

5. She will call her friend who is sick.

6. The small gray dog runs on the wall.

7. The red ball is up in the tree.

8. We will shop at the mall.

9. I should cut the grass.

10. He sells shells at his stall.

Dibuios

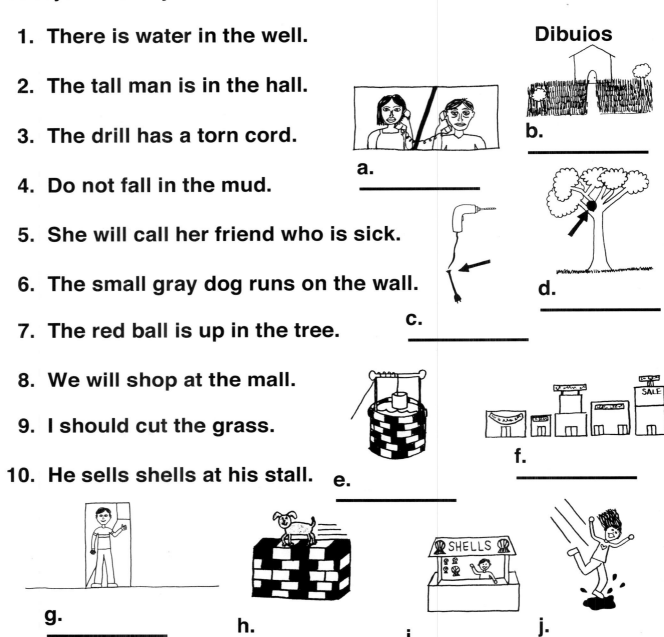

a.

b.

c.

d.

e.

f.

g.

h.

i.

j.

Spelling Dictation * Dictado

Pídale a alguien que le dicte las palabras de la página 30. Después de escribirlas, LÉALAS y revise la ortografía. Corrija las palabras que estén equivocadas.

Fill in the Blanks * Llene el Espacio

Llene cada espacio con una palabra de la lista de palabras. Use cada palabra solamente una vez. Algunas oraciones tienen dibujos al final para ayudarle.

1. She sells dresses at the _____ .

2. I wish you _____ give the speech.

3. The small cat sits on top of the brick _____ .

4. _____ I cut the ham?

5. The four kids play with the big red _____ .

6. The _____ dog swims at the bay.

7. She plays a big _____ horn.

8. There is not much water in the _____ .

9. She sells dolls at her _____ at the mall.

10. I will _____ my friend who lives in Mexico.

11. The _____ man does not fit in the van.

12. Do not _____ off the wall.

13. _____ you fry the eggs, please?

14. You need to plug in the _____ .

15. Do not track mud in the _____ .

Spelling Demons * Demonios de la ortografía

Las siguientes palabras que se usan con frecuencia a menudo se escriben con mala ortografía.

your	you're	would	what
some	of	my	from

Use las palabras anteriores en las oraciones a continuación. Use cada palabra una sola vez.

1. The eggs and ham are _____ Dan.

2. _____ of my checks are in the box.

3. _____ do you want to do?

4. _____ dad could cash the check here.

5. _____ truck is stuck in the mud.

6. She has a bag _____ chips.

7. _____ here for the quiz.

8. Where _____ they go?

Rhyming Words * Palabras que riman

Las palabras que riman son palabras que comienzan de manera diferente pero terminan con la misma vocal y los mismos sonidos en la terminación. Por ejemplo, *red, bed* y *said* son palabras que riman. No necesitan escribirse igual, pero necesitan terminar con la misma vocal y los mismos sonidos en la terminación.

Si las dos palabras riman, escriba "yes" (sí); si no, escriba "no" (no).

do	go	9. _____
well	wall	10. _____
brass	glass	11. _____
should	could	12. _____
chip	ship	13. _____

WordSearch * Busca Palabras

Encuentra las palabras de la Lección 5 en el busca palabras. Marca las respuestas. Las palabras pueden estar escritas en forma normal, al revés o diagonalmente.

	hall	small	tall
stall	brass	should	could
would			

c	o	u	l	d	f	a	l	l
s	p	f	a	l	l	i	r	d
t	q	y	t	l	l	a	m	s
a	h	a	l	l	d	w	b	n
l	s	a	u	l	l	o	t	s
l	z	s	u	v	l	u	l	l
i	r	o	a	i	a	l	l	l
t	h	m	w	r	t	d	a	a
s	m	a	l	l	b	t	b	c

29

Answer Key * Las Respuestas

Sentences * Oraciones (page 26)

a. 5	f. 8
b. 9	g. 2
c. 3	h. 6
d. 7	i. 10
e. 1	j. 4

Spelling Dictation * Dictado (page 26)

chip, so, who, track, sort, creek much, small, corn, shock, shy, wall, chick, me, what; My speech is on the mat. Can my friend play chess?

Fill in the Blanks * Llene el Espacio (page 27)

1.	mall	9.	stall
2.	could	10.	call
3.	wall	11.	tall
4.	Should	12.	fall
5.	ball	13.	Would
6.	small	14.	drill
7.	brass	15.	hall
8.	well		

Spelling Demons & Rhyming Words * Demonios de la ortografía y Palabras que riman (page 28)

1.	from	6.	of	11.	Yes
2.	Some	7.	You're	12.	Yes
3.	What	8.	would	13.	Yes
4.	My or Your	9.	No		
5.	Your or My	10.	No		

WordSearch * Busca Palabras (page 29)

Reading and Spelling Check #1
Verificación de lectura y escritura #1

Haga que alguien le dicte las siguientes palabras, leyéndolas por columnas. Escriba las palabras. Cuando haya terminado de escribirlas, léalas. Al pie de esta página, escriba tres veces las palabras que escribió mal. Busque en un diccionario todas las palabras cuyo significado no conozca.

storm	my	sport	grin
was	small	where	shed
slim	ship	stall	hall
green	plum	brick	creep
fluff	clock	fork	fresh

Lesson 6 * Lección 6

Word List * La lista de las palabras

Combine los sonidos de las letras para leer y entender la ortografía de las palabras. Las letras <u>th</u> tienen dos sonidos, uno que se pronuncia y otro que no se pronuncia. La combinación <u>th</u> se pronuncia /th/ como aparece en *that* o *thin*.

Inglés	Español
1. that	eso
2. thin	delgado
3. thick	grueso
4. then	entonces
5. them	ellos
6. math	matemáticas
7. with	con
8. bath	baño
9. cloth	paño
10. this	esto
11. thorn	espina
12. fourth	cuarto
13. fifth	quinto
14. sixth	sexto
15. tenth	décimo

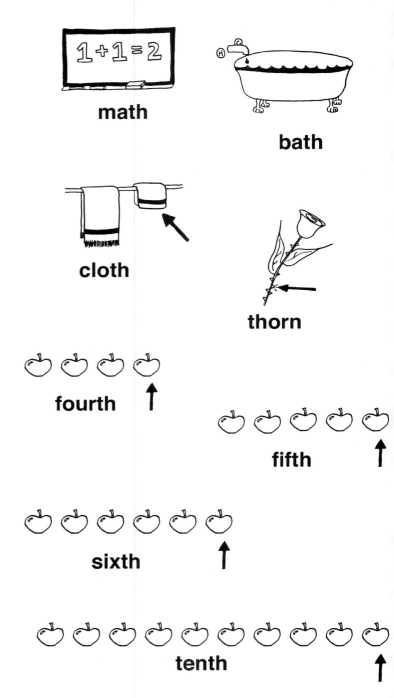

math

bath

cloth

thorn

fourth

fifth

sixth

tenth

Sentences * Oraciones

Lea las oraciones. Después escriba el número de la oración debajo del dibujo correcto.

1. The tall thin man chops the tree.

2. This stack is short.

3. The water in the bath is too hot.

4. That cloth is torn.

5. The dog has a thorn in its leg.

6. I will check your math.

7. She will give the small duck to them.

8. My red dish is the fourth one in the stack.

9. The green ball is with the bat.

10. This small pup was born today.

Dibujos

a. _____

b. _____

c. _____

d. _____

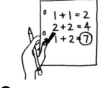

e. _____

g. _____

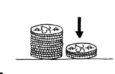

h. _____

i. _____

j. _____

Spelling Dictation * Dictado

Pídale a alguien que le dicte las palabras de la página 37. Después de escribirlas, LÉALAS y revise la ortografía. Corrija las palabras que estén equivocadas.

Fill in the Blanks * Llene el Espacio

Llene cada espacio con una palabra de la lista de palabras. Use cada palabra solamente una vez. Algunas oraciones tienen dibujos al final para ayudarle.

1. Please do not put your feet on the green _____ .

2. _____ small chick is for you.

3. The black pig is too _____ .

4. This is the _____ red van I have seen today.

5. _____ ham is too sweet.

6. She says _____ is fun.

7. We will sort the dishes and glasses for _____ .

8. Pam will be _____ to go.

9. Meg will go _____ her friend to the mall.

10. Do not step on the _____ .

11. There is a _____ fog today.

12. We will get water from the well for your _____ .

13. You will be the _____ one to give a speech.

14. You need to brush the dog and _____ you may go.

15. The _____ dog is too sick to run.

Possessives * Posesivos

Para indicar pertenencia debe añadir un apóstrofe y una <u>s</u> ('s) al sustantivo. Use las siguientes palabras para completar las oraciones. Recuerde añadir un apóstrofe y una <u>s</u> ('s) para indicar pertenencia.

drill	frog	friend	chick
mom	man	dad	Pam

Use las palabras anteriores en las oraciones a continuación. Use cada palabra una sola vez.

1. _____ van is in the street.

2. The _____ skin is too thick.

3. The _____ egg is still in the grass.

4. _____ dress has a brass pin.

5. My _____ neck is red from the sun.

6. The _____ cord is cut.

7. The _____ fork is by the corn.

8. Where is _____ lunch?

Rhyming Words * Palabras que riman

Las palabras que riman son palabras que comienzan de manera diferente pero terminan con la misma vocal y los mismos sonidos en la terminación. Por ejemplo, *red, bed* y *said* son palabras que riman. No necesitan escribirse igual, pero necesitan terminar con la misma vocal y los mismos sonidos en la terminación.

Escriba dos palabras que rimen con la palabra en la primera columna.

fed	9. _____	_____
ray	10. _____	_____
should	11. _____	_____
sell	12. _____	_____
mop	13. _____	_____

WordSearch * Busca Palabras

Encuentra las palabras de la Lección 6 en el busca palabras. Marca las respuestas. Las palabras pueden estar escritas en forma normal, al revés o diagonalmente.

			that
thin	**thick**	**then**	**them**
with	**this**		

s	i	x	t	h	m	h	m	k
s	i	h	t	h	t	i	l	c
k	y	f	t	r	t	o	f	i
b	y	h	u	f	b	o	p	h
k	i	o	i	m	t	a	l	t
n	f	f	a	t	n	a	t	c
p	t	t	h	n	b	e	h	h
h	h	e	h	t	i	w	h	t
m	m	s	h	t	n	e	t	t

Answer Key * Las Respuestas

Sentences * Oraciones (page 33)

a. 5

b. 7

c. 8

d. 10

e. 6

f. 4

g. 3

h. 2

i. 9

j. 1

Spelling Dictation * Dictado (page 33)

chat, tall, go, are, thin, drill, from, born, fish, chess, call, be, could, trap, clap;
Pam is tall and Bob is short. The big black ship is not in the port.

Fill in the Blanks * Llene el Espacio (page 34)

1. cloth
2. This or That
3. thin
4. fourth
5. That or This
6. math
7. them
8. fifth
9. with
10. thorn
11. thick
12. bath
13. tenth
14. then
15. sixth

Possessives & Rhyming Words * Posesivos y Palabras que riman (page 35)

1.	Dad's	5.	friend's
2.	frog's	6.	drill's
3.	chick's	7.	man's
4.	Pam's	8.	mom's

9. – 13. Answers will vary. Las respuestas pueden variar.

WordSearch * Busca Palabras (page 36)

Lesson 7 * Lección 7

Word List * Lista de palabras

Combine los sonidos de la consonante y la vocal para leer y entender la ortografía de las palabras. Las letras <u>ing</u> se pronuncian /ing/ como en *sing*, las letras <u>ang</u> se pronuncian /ang/ como en *sang*, las letras <u>ong</u> se pronuncian /ong/ como en *song*, y las letras <u>ung</u> se pronuncian /ung/ como en *sung*.

Inglés	Español
1. ring	anillo
2. wing	ala
3. bring	traer
4. thing	cosa
5. swing	columpio
6. hang	colgar
7. rang	sonó
8. bang	golpear
9. long	largo
10. song	canción
11. stung	picó
12. lung	pulmón
13. any	cualquiera
14. many	muchos
15. only	sólo

ring

wing

swing

lung

Sentences * Oraciones

Lea las oraciones. Después escriba el número de la oración debajo del dibujo correcto.

1. Meg will hang the blue dress on the peg.

2. His dad has only one lung.

3. Pat will play on the swing.

4. The bell rang at one o'clock.

5. The duck has a black wing.

6. The bee stung Sam on the leg.

7. Please bring the fork to me.

8. She sang a long song.

9. Please do not bang the pans.

10. My ring fell in the mud.

Dibujos

a. _____

b. _____

c. _____

d. _____

e. _____

f. _____

g. _____

h. _____

i. _____

j. _____

Spelling Dictation * Dictado

Pídale a alguien que le dicte las palabras de la página 43. Después de escribirlas, LÉALAS y revise la ortografía. Corrija las palabras que estén equivocadas.

Fill in the Blank * Llene el Espacio

Llene cada espacio con una palabra de la lista de palabras. Use cada palabra solamente una vez. Algunas oraciones tienen dibujos al final para ayudarle.

1. He will hang the _____ from the tree.

2. I have _____ one black dress.

3. Do you have _____ chips in your lunch?

4. That _____ is too big for the box.

5. My small black dog has only one _____ .

6. There are _____ big green bugs in the tree.

7. Please _____ the clock on the wall.

8. Do I have to sing a _____ ?

9. She has a _____ blue dress for the prom.

10. Please put the _____ in the small box.

11. What did you _____ for lunch?

12. Mom says do not _____ your truck on the wall.

13. The duck's _____ is in the trap.

14. He says the bee _____ the pig.

15. The bell _____ for lunch.

Spelling Demons * Demonios de la ortografía

Las siguientes palabras que se usan con frecuencia a menudo se escriben con mala ortografía.

when	win	than	then
some	do	until	something

Use las palabras anteriores en las oraciones a continuación. Use cada palabra una sola vez.

1. I am taller _____ my dad.

2. He has _____ in his van for you.

3. I want _____ chips for my snack.

4. Please _____ not ring the bell.

5. We will swim and _____ we will have lunch.

6. _____ will you floss your teeth?

7. We will not go _____ they come.

8. She wants to _____ the cash.

Rhyming Words * Palabras que riman

Las palabras que riman son palabras que comienzan de manera diferente pero terminan con la misma vocal y los mismos sonidos en la terminación. Por ejemplo, *red, bed* y *said* son palabras que riman. No necesitan escribirse igual, pero necesitan terminar con la misma vocal y los mismos sonidos en la terminación.

Escriba dos palabras que rimen con la primera palabra en cada renglón.

ring	9. _____	_____
hang	10. _____	_____
long	11. _____	_____
lung	12. _____	_____
sport	13. _____	_____

WordSearch * Busca Palabras

Encuentra las palabras de la Lección 7 en el busca palabras. Marca las respuestas. Las palabras pueden estar escritas en forma normal, al revés o diagonalmente.

any	**many**	**bring**	**only**
thing	**stung**	**hang**	**long**
rang	**bang**	**song**	

O	L	H	W	T	S	O	N	G
G	N	U	A	S	H	A	H	O
R	A	L	N	N	T	I	X	N
G	N	X	Y	G	G	U	N	F
N	Y	J	G	M	S	G	N	G
I	X	N	A	W	N	G	G	G
R	A	N	I	I	N	N	L	J
R	Y	N	R	A	O	N	Q	H
M	G	B	B	L	G	N	I	W

Answer Key * Las Respuestas

Sentences * Oraciones (page 39)

a. 2
b. 5
c. 8
d. 1
e. 10

f. 7
g. 4
h. 6
i. 3
j. 9

Spelling Dictation * Dictado (page 39)

with, ball, sting, your, frog, slang, slush, this, long, form, check, lung, thin, hall, fling; Dry the cup with a thick cloth. Who is in the shed?

Fill in the Blank * Llene el Espacio (page 40)

1. swing
2. only
3. any
4. thing
5. lung
6. many
7. hang
8. song

9. long
10. ring
11. bring
12. bang
13. wing
14. stung
15. rang

Spelling Demons & Rhyming Words * Demonios de la ortografía y Palabras que riman (page 41)

1.	than	5.	then
2.	something	6.	When
3.	some	7.	until
4.	do	8.	win

9. – 13. Answers will vary. Las respuestas pueden variar.

WordSearch * Busca Palabras (page 42)

Lesson 8 * Lección 8

Word List * Lista de palabras

Combine los sonidos de las letras para leer y entender la ortografía de las palabras. Las letras <u>oy</u> se pronuncian /oy/ como en *boy*. Regla: las letras <u>oy</u> generalmente se encuentran al final de una palabra. Las letras <u>ar</u> se pronuncian /ar/ como en *car*.

Inglés	Español
1. boy	niño
2. toy	juguete
3. joy	alegría
4. car	automóvil
5. dark	oscuro
6. farm	granja
7. park	parque
8. march	marchar
9. sharp	puntiagudo
10. hard	duro
11. far	lejos
12. star	estrella
13. card	tarjeta
14. smart	inteligente
15. yard	patio

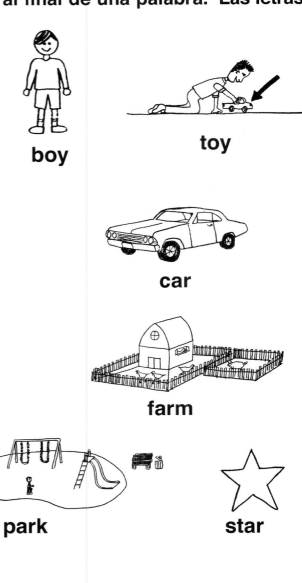

boy

toy

car

farm

park

star

card

yard

Sentences * Oraciones

Lea las oraciones. Después escriba el número de la oración debajo del dibujo correcto.

1. The thin boy will march at the park.

2. She will feel joy when she sees them.

3. The toy truck is in the yard.

4. He will park the car at the club.

5. We will get many eggs at the farm.

6. When it's dark, we can see the stars.

7. The dog has a sharp thorn in its leg.

8. Do not sit on the hard rock.

9. Where is the card for mom?

10. The ducks are far from the water.

Dibujos

a.

b.

c.

d.

e.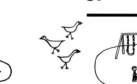

f.

g.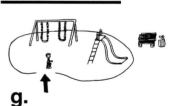

h.

i.

j.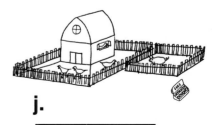

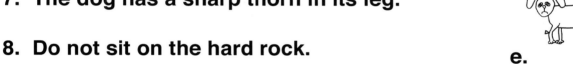

Spelling Dictation * Dictado

Pídale a alguien que le dicte las palabras de la página 49. Después de escribirlas, LÉALAS y revise la ortografía. Corrija las palabras que estén equivocadas.

Fill in the Blank * Llene el Espacio

Llene cada espacio con una palabra de la lista de palabras. Use cada palabra solamente una vez. Algunas oraciones tienen dibujos al final para ayudarle.

1. Do not step on the glass in the _____.

2. The long thorn is _____.

3. The boys play on the swing in the _____.

4. The _____ boy does the hard math.

5. I will park my _____ at the mall.

6. She will _____ and play the drum.

7. The _____ truck will cheer up the boy.

8. It was _____ in the shed.

9. The pigs live on the _____.

10. The small boy will give them _____.

11. There is a small red _____ on the black cloth.

12. Their pup is _____ from the fort.

13. He will give a _____ and a kiss to his mom.

14. That is a _____ song to sing.

15. The fifth _____ has a thick neck.

46

Making New Words * Formación de nuevas palabras

Quite el sonido final de cada palabra para formar una nueva palabra.

Original Word	New Word
farm	1. _____
start	2. _____
card	3. _____
fourth	4. _____
says	5. _____
fort	6. _____
think	7. _____
fork	8. _____
tenth	9. _____
shell	10. _____
and	11. _____

Quite la última letra de cada palabra para formar una nueva palabra.

Original Word	New Word
wing	12. _____
thing	13. _____
rang	14. _____
one	15. _____
they	16. _____
your	17. _____

WordSearch * Busca Palabras

Encuentra las palabras de la Lección 8 en el busca palabras. Marca las respuestas. Las palabras pueden estar escritas en forma normal, al revés o diagonalmente.

	joy	dark	march
sharp	far	start	hard

U	V	S	J	C	F	D	P
A	S	O	A	A	R	R	E
S	Y	R	R	A	A	O	D
S	M	M	C	H	H	S	R
K	T	A	S	S	Y	W	A
X	R	A	R	B	R	O	H
Y	F	A	R	C	O	A	T
N	L	K	D	T	H	Y	F

Answer Key * Las Respuestas

Sentences * Oraciones (page 45)

a. 3
b. 8
c. 6
d. 9
e. 7

f. 10
g. 1
h. 2
i. 4
j. 5

Spelling Dictation * Dictado (page 45)

thing, mall, whale, you, crib, toy, flick, them, farm, rang, much, song, who;
Meg had a long run up the hill. Hang the dress on the peg.

Fill in the Blank * Llene el Espacio (page 46)

1. yard
2. sharp
3. park
4. smart
5. car
6. march
7. toy
8. dark

9. farm
10. joy
11. star
12. far
13. card
14. hard
15. boy

Making New Words * Formación de nuevas palabras (page 47)

1.	far	10.	she
2.	star	11.	an
3.	car	12.	win
4.	four	13.	thin
5.	say	14.	ran
6.	for	15.	on
7.	thin	16.	the
8.	for	17.	you
9.	ten		

WordSearch * Busca Palabras (page 48)

49

Lesson 9 * Lección 9

Word List * Lista de palabras

Combine los sonidos de la consonante y la vocal para leer y entender la ortografía de las palabras. Las letras <u>wh</u> se pronuncian /wh/ como en *wheel*. Regla: Las letras <u>wh</u> aparecen al principio de una palabra. En la mayoría de los lugares en Estados Unidos, las letras <u>wh</u> y la letra <u>w</u> suenan de la misma manera.

Inglés	Español
1. when	cuándo
2. whip	látigo
3. wheel	rueda
4. why	por qué
5. whiz	genio
6. which	cuál
7. whiff	olorcillo
8. whack	golpear
9. whim	capricho
10. whose	de quién
11. what	qué
12. where	dónde
13. who	quién
14. was	estaba
15. were	estaban estábamos

whip

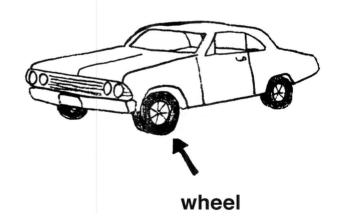

wheel

Sentences * Oraciones

Lea las oraciones. Después escriba el número de la oración debajo del dibujo correcto.

1. Please do not whack the bat on the tree.

2. Whose car is in your yard?

3. When did your dad bring the drill?

4. We were at the park.

5. Where is your mom's farm?

6. Which ring do you want?

7. She is a whiz in math.

8. The van has four thick wheels.

9. Who was at the mall?

10. What is in the small box?

Dibujos

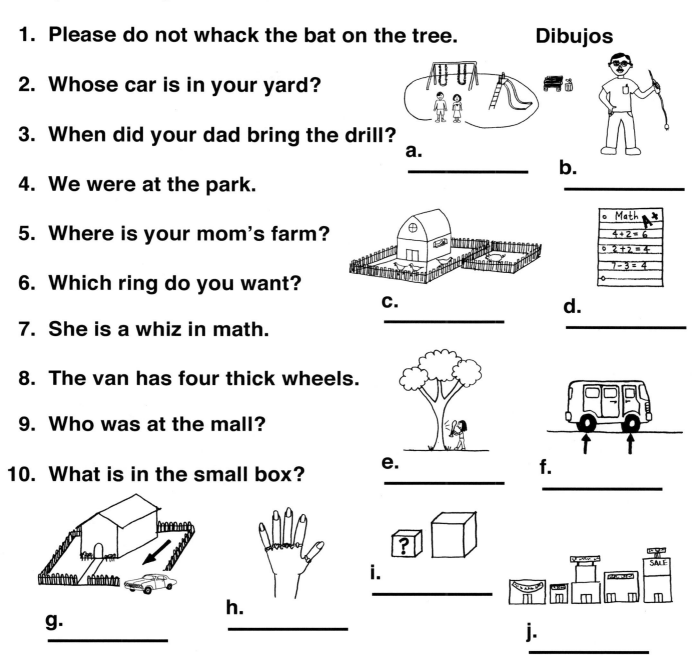

a. _____

b. _____

c. _____

d. _____

e. _____

f. _____

g. _____

h. _____

i. _____

j. _____

Spelling Dictation * Dictado

Pídale a alguien que le dicte las palabras de la página 55. Después de escribirlas, LÉALAS y revise la ortografía. Corrija las palabras que estén equivocadas.

Fill in the Blanks * Llene el Espacio

Llene cada espacio con una palabra de la lista de palabras. Use cada palabra solamente una vez. Algunas oraciones tienen dibujos al final para ayudarle.

1. Did you get a _____ of the ham?

2. We will pay cash for the big _____ .

3. _____ way do you want to go?

4. The fourth boy is a _____ in chess.

5. _____ will bring the chips?

6. _____ you with them?

7. _____ is the card for mom?

8. As a _____ we ran in the mud.

9. Do not _____ the log with the ax.

10. _____ will you go to the farm?

11. _____ is your car in the shed?

12. _____ red ball is in the hall?

13. Do not _____ the dog with the stick.

14. _____ do you want for lunch?

15. He _____ at the park with his dog.

Question Sentences * Preguntas

Escriba preguntas usando cada una de las siguientes palabras.

when	why	which	whose
what	where	who	how

1. _____

2. _____

3. _____

4. _____

5. _____

6. _____

7. _____

8. _____

Making New Words * Formación de nuevas palabras

Quite la primera letra en la palabra original para formar una nueva palabra. Hicimos la primera palabra para usted.

Original Word	New Word
whim	9. _____ *him* _____
what	10. _____
where	11. _____
when	12. _____
the	13. _____
his	14. _____
for	15. _____
has	16. _____
there	17. _____
was	18. _____

WordSearch * Busca Palabras

Encuentra las palabras de la Lección 9 en el busca palabras. Marca las respuestas. Las palabras pueden estar escritas en forma normal, al revés o diagonalmente.

		when	why
whiz	which	whiff	whack
whim	where	who	was
what	were		

T	C	S	Z	I	H	W	W	K
P	A	X	A	Q	U	H	C	F
H	T	H	L	W	O	A	G	F
C	J	S	W	E	H	Z	D	I
I	W	Z	W	W	E	W	M	H
H	J	H	E	N	W	H	H	W
W	I	R	E	S	E	H	W	Y
P	E	H	I	A	Y	Z	I	I
W	W	I	E	R	E	H	W	M

54

Answer Key * Las Respuestas

Sentences * Oraciones (page 51)

a. 4
b. 3
c. 5
d. 7
e. 1

f. 8
g. 2
h. 6
i. 10
j. 9

Spelling Dictation * Dictado (page 51)

sting, short, wheel, was, crack, joy, flock, thick, star, bang, chop, long, where, bring, horn; Bring your math with you. She said you were sick.

Fill in the Blanks * Llene el Espacio (page 52)

1. whiff
2. wheel
3. Which
4. whiz
5. Who
6. Were
7. Where
8. whim

9. whack
10. When
11. Why
12. Whose
13. whip
14. What
15. was

Question Sentences & Making New Words * Preguntas y Formación de nuevas palabras (page 53)

1. – 8. Answers will vary. Las respuestas pueden variar.

9.	him	14.	is
10.	hat	15.	or
11.	here	16.	as
12.	hen	17.	here
13.	he	18.	as

WordSearch * Busca Palabras (page 54)

Lesson 10 * Lección 10

Word List * Lista de palabras

Combine los sonidos de la consonante y la vocal para leer y entender la ortografía de las palabras. Regla: la letra **–k** es la letra preferida para el sonido /k/ al final de una palabra después de una consonante, una vocal larga o una doble vocal. Las letras **–ck** aparecen al final de una palabra después de una vocal corta.

Inglés	Español
1. pink	rosa
2. sink	fregadero
3. think	pensar
4. drink	beber
5. bank	banco
6. sank	hundió
7. thank	agradecer
8. drank	bebió
9. blank	espacio en blanco
10. honk	sonar la bocina
11. trunk	baúl
12. bunk	litera
13. very	muy
14. don't	verbo auxiliar para formar el negativo

sink

bank

trunk

bunk

56

Sentences * Oraciones

Lea las oraciones. Después escriba el número de la oración debajo del dibujo correcto.

1. Please put the small pink dress in the trunk.

2. The cash is in the bank.

3. I will sleep on the top bunk.

4. Thank you for the hot drink.

5. Did Pat win a van?

6. The rock sank in the water.

7. Do not honk the horn.

8. He drank a tall glass of water.

9. The dishes are in the sink.

10. He says to fill in the blank.

Dibujos

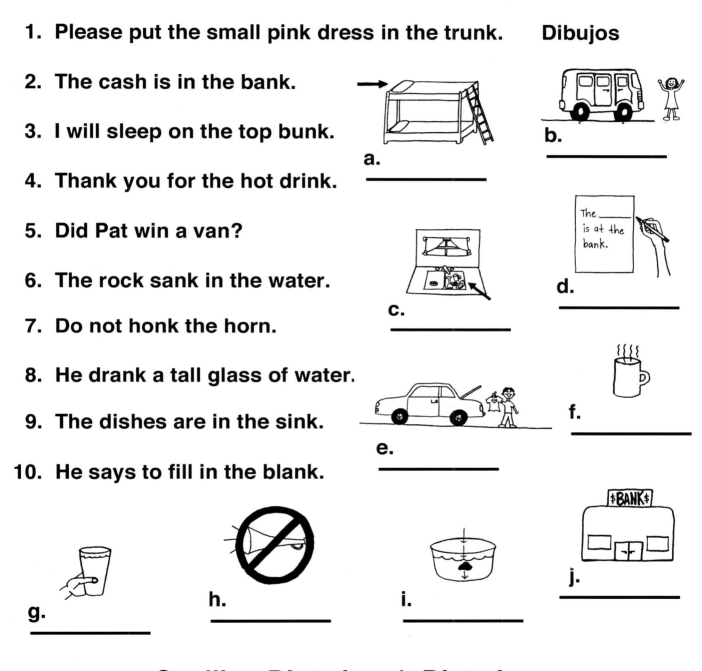

a. ____

b. ____

c. ____

d. ____

e. ____

f. ____

g. ____

h. ____

i. ____

j. ____

Spelling Dictation * Dictado

Pídale a alguien que le dicte las palabras de la página 61. Después de escribirlas, LÉALAS y revise la ortografía. Corrija las palabras que estén equivocadas.

Fill in the Blank * Llene el Espacio

Llene cada espacio con una palabra de la lista de palabras. Use cada palabra solamente una vez. Algunas oraciones tienen dibujos al final para ayudarle.

1. My friend's _____ dress is wet.

2. The balls and bats are in the _____ .

3. Please _____ grab the map.

4. I will cash my check at the _____ .

5. Who _____ all the water?

6. Do not stack the cups in the _____ .

7. _____ your horn at the cab.

8. She will fill in the _____ .

9. _____ you for the red rug.

10. We will _____ water for lunch.

11. Who will sleep on the top _____ ?

12. I _____ I will have the beef for lunch.

13. That hill is _____ steep.

14. He can't swim. He _____ in the water.

58

Vocabulary * Vocabulario

Use las palabras que aparecen a continuación para llenar los espacios en blanco. Es posible que necesite usar un diccionario.

think	thing	ring	rink
sink	sing	wing	wink
bank	bang	sang	sank

1. The truck _____ in the water.

2. The checks are at the _____ .

3. The kids will play at the _____ .

4. Tim can not swim. He will _____ in the water.

5. What is that flat green _____ ?

6. The _____ for Meg is in the small pink box.

7. Tom will be the tenth boy to _____ the song.

8. She will _____ at the boy.

9. Did you hear the _____ ?

10. The duck's _____ is red and black.

11. The small boy _____ a very long song.

12. I _____ the cat is sick.

WordSearch * Busca Palabras

Encuentra las palabras de la Lección 10 en el busca palabras. Marca las respuestas. Las palabras pueden estar escritas en forma normal, al revés o diagonalmente.

		pink	think
drink		drank	thank
blank	honk		

D	H	O	K	N	A	H	T
D	R	T	R	U	N	K	M
Z	D	I	B	A	N	K	N
K	B	R	N	P	U	J	B
N	U	K	A	K	Z	L	R
I	N	N	G	N	A	K	H
H	K	I	C	N	K	T	O
T	Y	P	K	H	O	N	K

Answer Key * Las Respuestas

Sentences * Oraciones (page 57)

a. 3
b. 5
c. 9
d. 10
e. 1

f. 4
g. 8
h. 7
i. 6
j. 2

Spelling Dictation * Dictado (page 57)

sung, stall, pink, one, when, far, bank, black, think, honk, torch, yard, only, spy, boy; Play with the toy in the yard. That is a sharp rock.

Fill in the Blank * Llene el Espacio (page 58)

1. pink
2. trunk
3. don't
4. bank
5. drank
6. sink
7. Honk

8. blank
9. Thank
10. drink
11. bunk
12. think
13. very
14. sank

Vocabulary * Vocabulario (page 59)

1.	sank	7.	sing
2.	bank	8.	wink
3.	rink	9.	bang
4.	sink	10.	wing
5.	thing	11.	sang
6.	ring	12.	think

WordSearch * Busca Palabras (page 60)

Reading and Spelling Check #2
Verificación de lectura y escritura #2

Haga que alguien le dicte las siguientes palabras, leyéndolas por columnas. Escriba las palabras. Cuando haya terminado de escribirlas, léalas. Al pie de esta página, escriba tres veces las palabras que escribió mal. Busque en un diccionario todas las palabras cuyo significado no conozca.

which	thank	trunk	pray
corn	would	joy	form
shark	start	many	chick
clang	lock	sheep	from
were	that	stiff	long

Lesson 11 * Lección 11

Word List * Lista de palabras

Combine los sonidos de la consonante y la vocal para leer y entender la ortografía de las palabras. Las letras <u>oo</u> se pronuncian /oo/ como en *food*. Regla: las letras <u>oo</u> a menudo aparecen a la mitad de una palabra.

Inglés	Español
1. food	alimento
2. moon	luna
3. soon	pronto
4. spoon	cuchara
5. boot	bota
6. cool	fresco
7. tool	herramienta
8. pool	piscina
9. broom	escoba
10. zoo	zoológico
11. booth	caseta
12. tooth	diente
13. once	una vez
14. our	nuestro

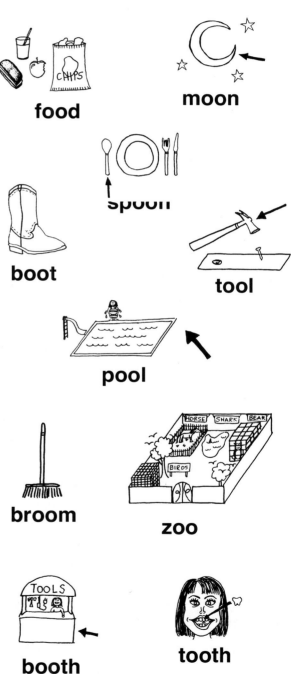

food

moon

spoon

boot

tool

pool

broom

zoo

booth

tooth

Sentences * Oraciones

Lea las oraciones. Después escriba el número de la oración debajo del dibujo correcto.

1. Please bring the food to the mat.

2. Where is your black boot?

3. Soon the corn will be tall.

4. The water in the pool is cool.

5. Meg's fourth tooth fell out.

6. We will go to the zoo soon.

7. Our toys are in the park.

8. We will sell our tools at the booth.

9. The broom fell on the cat.

10. When we sit in the tree, we can see the moon.

Dibujos

a. _____

b. _____

c. _____

d. _____

e. _____

f. _____

g. _____

h. _____

i. _____

j. _____

Spelling Dictation * Dictado

Pídale a alguien que le dicte las palabras de la página 68. Después de escribirlas, **LÉALAS** y revise la ortografía. Corrija las palabras que estén equivocadas.

Fill in the Blank * Llene el Espacio

Llene cada espacio con una palabra de la lista de palabras. Use cada palabra solamente una vez. Algunas oraciones tienen dibujos al final para ayudarle.

1. Were there many ducks at the _____ ?

2. Dan wants to swim in the _____ .

3. _____ dad is sick in bed.

4. We will meet at the food _____ .

5. There is a lot of _____ for lunch.

6. The small pink _____ is in the sink.

7. Mom put a _____ cloth on Meg's bee sting.

8. The tools and _____ are in the shed.

9. Please put my _____ in a bag.

10. Our friends will be here _____ .

11. There is a red _____ in the hall.

12. I need a sharp _____ .

13. _____ you're in bed, I will give you a drink.

14. I can see the _____ from my bed.

Making New Words * Formación de nuevas palabras

Quite una letra de la palabra original para formar una nueva palabra. Hicimos la primera para usted.

Original Word		New Word
spoon	1.	*soon*
our	2.	
bring	3.	
once	4.	
drank	5.	
whip	6.	
drink	7.	

Homophones * Homófonos

Una palabra homófona es una que suena como otra pero que tiene diferente ortografía y significado. Los siguientes homófonos están entre las palabras que se escriben más a menudo con mala ortografía en el idioma inglés.

their	there	they're
you're	your	
its	it's	

Escriba oraciones correctamente con cada homófono.

8. _____

9. _____

10. _____

11. _____

12. _____

13. _____

14. _____

WordSearch * Busca Palabras

Encuentra las palabras de la Lección 11 en el busca palabras. Marca las respuestas. Las palabras pueden estar escritas en forma normal, al revés o diagonalmente.

D	O	O	F	M	R	T	B
F	O	Y	O	U	E	O	O
Z	H	O	O	R	C	O	O
S	R	T	Z	I	N	T	T
B	B	N	O	O	O	H	L
M	O	O	N	O	O	I	O
T	L	O	O	C	B	G	O
S	P	O	O	N	I	Z	P

Answer Key * Las Respuestas

Sentences * Oraciones (page 64)

a. 3
b. 7
c. 5
d. 4
e. 8

f. 1
g. 2
h. 10
i. 9
j. 6

Spelling Dictation * Dictado (page 64)

blink, storm, rink, here, why, sharp, tank, slick, cloth, bunk, chap, tooth, part, long, dorm; Do not fling the food. Which dog can go?

Fill in the Blank * Llene el Espacio (page 65)

1. zoo
2. pool
3. Our
4. booth
5. food
6. spoon
7. cool

8. broom
9. tooth
10. soon
11. boot
12. tool
13. Once
14. moon

Making New Words and Homophones * Formación de nuevas palabras y Homófonos (page 66)

1.	soon	5.	rank
2.	or	6.	hip
3.	ring	7.	rink
4.	one		

8. – 14. Answers will vary. Las respuestas pueden variar.

WordSearch * Busca Palabras (page 67)

D	O	O	F	M	R	T	B
F	O	Y	O	U	E	O	O
Z	H	O	O	R	C	O	O
S	R	T	Z	I	N	T	T
B	B	N	O	O	O	H	L
M	O	O	N	O	O	I	O
T	L	O	O	C	B	G	O
S	P	O	O	N	I	Z	P

Lesson 12 * Lección 12

Word List * Lista de palabras

La letra e al final de una palabra hace que la vocal que la precede diga su nombre. Ésta es la secuencia vocal-consonante-e.

Inglés	Español
1. dime	moneda de diez centavos
2. hope	esperanza
3. pine	pino
4. note	nota
5. slide	tobogán/resbalarse
6. spine	columna vertebral
7. made	hizo
8. bite	morder
9. hide	esconder
10. robe	bata
11. ripe	maduro
12. cube	cubo
13. been	estado
14. gone	ido

dime

note

slide

spine

robe

cube

Sentences * Oraciones

Lea las oraciones. Después escriba el número de la oración debajo del dibujo correcto.

1. The boy's mom gave him a dime for his tooth.   Dibujos

2. Don't let the dog bite you.

3. They have a big pine tree in their yard.

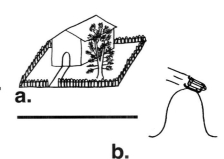
a. _____

4. The note from dad is on the wall.

b. _____

5. We will slide down the hill on our sled.

6. Mom will check your spine.

c. _____

7. Dad made a swing for the tree.

8. Please put the robe in the bathroom.

e. _____

9. Here is a ripe lime.

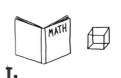
d. _____

10. We will use the cube for math.

f. _____

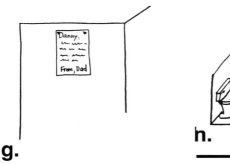
g. _____

h. _____

i. _____

j. _____

Spelling Dictation * Dictado

Pídale a alguien que le dicte las palabras de la página 74. Después de escribirlas, LÉALAS y revise la ortografía. Corrija las palabras que estén equivocadas.

Fill in the Blank * Llene el Espacio

Llene cada espacio con una palabra de la lista de palabras. Use cada palabra solamente una vez. Algunas oraciones tienen dibujos al final para ayudarle.

1. Do not step on my _____ .

2. The dog has been _____ for a long time.

3. The sixth _____ is red and black.

4. He will _____ the tools in the box.

5. The toy truck was made of _____ .

6. I will pay for it with a _____ .

7. I smell _____ plums.

8. Where have you _____ ?

9. Your blue _____ is in the bathroom.

10. I _____ you can go on the trip.

11. Dad _____ lunch for Sam and me.

12. Here is a thank you _____
_____ .

13. The little dog will _____ .

14. Do not run up the _____ .

71

Making New Words * Formación de nuevas palabras

Añada una <u>e</u> muda al final de cada palabra para formar una nueva palabra.

Original Word	New Word
dim	1. _____
cub	2. _____
rip	3. _____
rob	4. _____
pin	5. _____
not	6. _____
bit	7. _____
hid	8. _____
mad	9. _____
spin	10. _____
slid	11. _____
hop	12. _____

Writing Sentences * Oraciones para escribir

Escriba oraciones con las siguientes palabras. No olvide comenzar la oración con una letra mayúscula y terminarla con uno de los tres signos de puntación (. ? !).

mad	made	rip	ripe
rob	robe	dim	dime

13. _____

14. _____

15. _____

16. _____

17. _____

18. _____

19. _____

20. _____

WordSearch * Busca Palabras

Encuentra las palabras de la Lección 12 en el busca palabras. Marca las respuestas. Las palabras pueden estar escritas en forma normal, al revés o diagonalmente.

	bite	**hope**	**made**
hide	**been**	**gone**	

a	b	e	n	o	g	e	t
b	r	e	g	e	n	e	i
z	e	v	d	i	p	t	u
e	p	y	p	i	q	o	e
b	o	s	b	b	l	n	m
u	h	i	o	v	e	s	i
c	t	e	d	a	m	e	d
e	w	m	e	d	i	h	n

Answer Key * Las Respuestas

Sentences * Oraciones (page 70)

a.	3	f.	10
b.	5	g.	4
c.	9	h.	8
d.	1	i.	7
e.	2	j.	6

Spelling Dictation * Dictado (page 70)

junk, fort, what, dim, dime, were, soon, blink, yard, not, note, bloom, math, porch, star; Pam has one pink dress. When will we go to the park?

Fill in the Blank * Llene el Espacio (page 71)

1.	spine	8.	been
2.	gone	9.	robe
3.	cube	10.	hope
4.	hide	11.	made
5.	pine	12.	note
6.	dime	13.	bite
7.	ripe	14.	slide

Making New Words & Writing Sentences * Formación de nuevas palabras y Oraciones para escribir (page 72)

1.	dime	7.	bite
2.	cube	8.	hide
3.	ripe	9.	made
4.	robe	10.	spine
5.	pine	11.	slide
6.	note	12.	hope

13. – 20. Answers will vary. Las respuestas pueden variar.

WordSearch * Busca Palabras (page 73)

Lesson 13 * Lección 13

Word List * Lista de palabras

Las primeras doce palabras terminan en mezclas. Estas mezclas son los dos últimos sonidos consonantes en cada palabra.

Inglés	Español
1. last	último
2. best	mejor
3. fast	rápido
4. must	deber
5. hand	mano
6. pond	estanque
7. send	enviar
8. stand	estar de pie
9. went	el pasado del verbo *ir*
10. tent	tienda de campaña
11. rent	renta
12. spent	gastar dinero/pasar
13. everyone	todos
14. really	muy

hand

pond

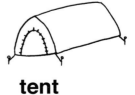

tent

Sentences * Oraciones

Lea las oraciones. Después escriba el número de la oración debajo del dibujo correcto.

1. She spent two dimes for gum.

2. Did everyone sing with Pam?

3. Meg has a very fast car.

4. That is a really big trunk.

5. You must stand in line.

6. They will sleep in a big tent.

7. We will send the box to Mom.

8. You must sit here.

9. There are six fish in the pond.

10. The boys went to the big park.

Dibujos

a. _____

b. _____

c. _____

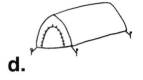

d. _____

e. _____

f. _____

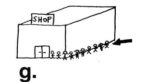

g. _____

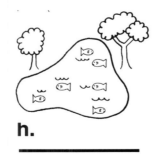

h. _____

i. _____

j. _____

Spelling Dictation * Dictado

Pídale a alguien que le dicte las palabras de la página 80. Después de escribirlas, **LÉALAS** y revise la ortografía. Corrija las palabras que estén equivocadas.

76

Fill in the Blank * Llene el Espacio

Llene cada espacio con una palabra de la lista de palabras. Use cada palabra solamente una vez. Algunas oraciones tienen dibujos al final para ayudarle.

1. Let's hide in the _____.

2. He _____ his time at the races.

3. Bill is the _____ one to finish his math.

4. Please put the ring in my _____.

5. We will pay the _____ on time.

6. The bank is _____ far from our home.

7. Mom makes the _____ food!

8. Sam and Ed _____ to the pool for a swim.

9. Please _____ by the tall tree.

10. Dad and Tom will fish at the _____.

11. Pat _____ have gone home.

12. We will _____ the tools to Bob.

13. _____ will play at the park.

14. The pig can run as _____ as the dog.

Compound Words * Las palabras compuestas

Las palabras compuestas contienen dos palabras pequeñas para formar una palabra. Use dos palabras pequeñas para formar una palabra compuesta.

Small Word	Small Word	Compound Word
sun	tan	1. _____
bath	tub	2. _____
sun	set	3. _____
sub	way	4. _____
pay	check	5. _____
pan	cake	6. _____
pop	corn	7. _____
rose	bud	8. _____
cup	cake	9. _____
bed	room	10. _____

Escriba siete oraciones con una palabra compuesta diferente en cada una.

11. _____

12. _____

13. _____

14. _____

15. _____

16. _____

17. _____

WordSearch * Busca Palabras

Encuentra las palabras de la Lección 13 en el busca palabras. Marca las respuestas. Las palabras pueden estar escritas en forma normal, al revés o diagonalmente.

			last
best	**fast**	**must**	**send**
really	**rent**	**spent**	**stand**
every			

f	l	v	c	t	n	e	p	s
t	a	y	s	e	n	d	e	p
g	s	s	l	g	h	v	t	h
i	t	a	t	l	e	d	a	g
d	n	o	l	r	a	n	y	t
n	e	c	y	b	d	e	q	n
o	t	o	e	s	i	p	r	e
p	n	s	m	u	s	t	l	r
e	t	x	r	d	n	a	t	s

Answer Key * Las Respuestas

Sentences * Oraciones (page 76)

a. 4

b. 7

c. 2

d. 6

e. 1

f. 3

g. 5

h. 9

i. 8

j. 10

Spelling Dictation * Dictado (page 76)

pin, pine, hung, fist, when, stoop, charm, two, mad, made, sand, goes, spin, spine, think; Did you bring the rope? I hope she can fix the bike.

Fill in the Blank * Llene el Espacio (page 77)

1. tent
2. spent
3. last
4. hand
5. rent
6. really
7. best
8. went
9. stand
10. pond
11. must
12. send
13. Everyone
14. fast

Compound Words * Las palabras compuestas (page 78)

1. suntan	6. pancake
2. bathtub	7. popcorn
3. sunset	8. rosebud
4. subway	9. cupcake
5. paycheck	10. bedroom

11. – 17. Answers will vary. Las respuestas pueden variar.

WordSearch * Busca Palabras (page 79)

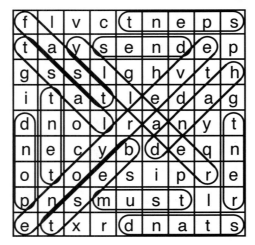

Lesson 14 * Lección 14

Word List * Lista de palabras

Las primeras doce palabras terminan en mezclas. Estas mezclas son los dos últimos sonidos consonantes en cada palabra.

Inglés	Español
1. lamp	lámpara
2. camp	campamento
3. pump	bomba/inflar
4. limp	cojera
5. ask	pedir
6. mask	máscara
7. tusk	colmillo
8. risk	riesgo
9. lift	levantar
10. left	dejó
11. craft	artesanía
12. gift	regalo
13. other	otro
14. buy	comprar

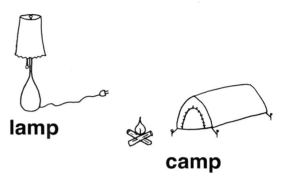

lamp

camp

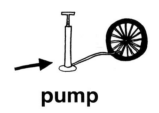

pump

mask

tusk

gift

Sentences * Oraciones

Lea las oraciones. Después escriba el número de la oración debajo del dibujo correcto.

1. We will set up camp on top of the hill.
2. Please pack the lamp in the box.
3. Bill has a mask on his face.
4. She gave the gift to Jan.
5. Sal will pump up the bike tire.
6. We will ask Pam for the tusk.
7. Meg will buy the pink robe.
8. The trunk is too heavy to lift.
9. She made a craft for your gift.
10. I will send the other card to Liz.

Dibujos

a. _____

b. _____

c. _____

d. _____

e. _____

f. _____

h. _____

i. _____

g. _____

j. _____

Spelling Dictation * Dictado

Pídale a alguien que le dicte las palabras de la página 86. Después de escribirlas, LÉALAS y revise la ortografía. Corrija las palabras que estén equivocadas.

Fill in the Blank * Llene el Espacio

Llene cada espacio con una palabra de la lista de palabras. Use cada palabra solamente una vez. Algunas oraciones tienen dibujos al final para ayudarle.

1. At _____ we will sleep in bunkbeds.

2. Al made a _____ for his mom's gift.

3. He wore a _____ to hide his face.

4. We will _____ ripe plums for lunch.

5. The brass _____ is in the hall.

6. The _____ mule is in the barn.

7. Meg will take a _____ when she buys the stocks.

8. The white _____ is very long and sharp.

9. The small dog runs with a _____ .

10. He _____ his rod at the pond.

11. Dad's _____ was a red car.

12. Sam will _____ his mom for a fork.

13. Please put the _____ by the wall.

14. Bill can _____ the big boxes and put them in the trunk.

Spelling Demons * Demonios de la ortografía

Las siguientes palabras que se usan con frecuencia a menudo se escriben con mala ortografía.

buy	have to	really	because
which	other	through	every

Use las palabras anteriores en las oraciones a continuación. Use cada palabra una sola vez.

1. We drove _____ the storm.

2. We _____ buy six lamps.

3. That car is _____ too small.

4. I will go _____ Mom wants me to be there.

5. Where is the _____ dog?

6. _____ pond has more fish?

7. It seems like she has _____ toy.

8. Dad will _____ a gift for Mom.

Words Ending in S * Palabras que terminan en la letra s

A veces, cuando una palabra termina en s, la s sonará como /z/. Indique si cada s suena como /s/ o /z/. La primera palabra ya se ha indicado.

Word	Sound for S	Word	Sound for S
9. as	/z/	14. hats	_____
10. bus	_____	15. rocks	_____
11. clams	_____	16. his	_____
12. has	_____	17. is	_____
13. dolls	_____	18. camps	_____

WordSearch * Busca Palabras

Encuentra las palabras de la Lección 14 en el busca palabras. Marca las respuestas. Las palabras pueden estar escritas en forma normal, al revés o diagonalmente.

	limp	ask	lift
left	craft	other	buy

L	A	P	G	L	V	S	N
I	P	S	C	T	E	U	Q
M	U	Q	K	R	F	F	E
P	M	Z	L	O	A	I	T
H	P	I	T	C	P	F	G
K	F	H	A	M	Y	T	T
T	E	M	A	U	V	N	V
R	P	L	B	M	A	S	K

Answer Key * Las Respuestas

Sentences * Oraciones (page 82)

a. 3
b. 10
c. 4
d. 8
e. 2

f. 9
g. 5
h. 7
i. 6
j. 1

Spelling Dictation * Dictado (page 82)

bit, bite, lung, dust, which, broom, smart, stamp, does, win, wine, send, could, cut, cute; Sell the shells at your booth. Peg will hide in the barn.

Fill in the Blank * Llene el Espacio (page 83)

1. camp
2. craft
3. mask
4. buy
5. lamp
6. other
7. risk

8. tusk
9. limp
10. left
11. gift
12. ask
13. pump
14. lift

Spelling Demons & Words Ending in <u>S</u> * Demonios de la ortografía y Palabras que terminan en la letra <u>s</u> (page 84)

1. through
2. have to
3. really
4. because
5. other

6. Which
7. every
8. buy
9. z
10. s

11. z
12. z
13. z
14. s
15. s

16. z
17. z
18. s

WordSearch * Busca Palabras (page 85)

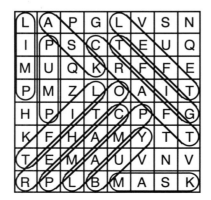

Lesson 15 * Lección 15

Word List * Lista de palabras

Las primeras doce palabras terminan en <u>ow</u>. En esta lista las letras <u>ow</u> forman el sonido de /o/ larga como en *low*. Regla: las letras <u>ow</u> aparecen al final de una palabra, o pueden ser seguidas por una <u>n</u>.

Inglés	Español
1. low	bajo
2. show	mostrar
3. blow	soplar
4. slow	despacio
5. snow	nieve
6. grow	crecer
7. own	poseer
8. grown	crecido
9. window	ventana
10. shadow	sombra
11. yellow	amarillo
12. follow	seguir
13. every	cada
14. done	terminado

slow

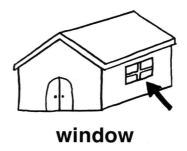

window

shadow

Sentences * Oraciones

Lea las oraciones. Después escriba el número de la oración debajo del dibujo correcto.

1. Please close the window.

2. The corn has grown tall.

3. The dog will follow me.

4. There is snow on your car.

5. Please show me your best smile.

6. Do not step on my shadow.

7. That truck goes too slow.

8. Every spoon has a K on it.

9. Do you own a big trunk?

10. Do you want the yellow or pink dress?

Dibujos

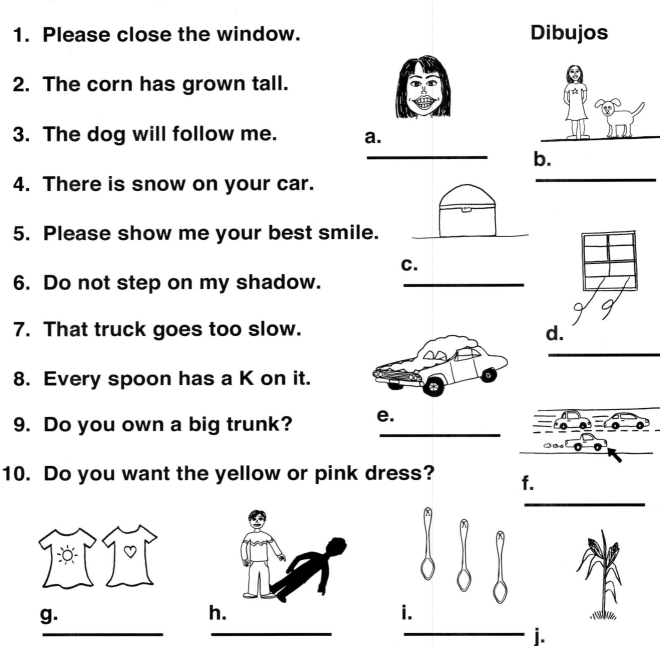

a. _____

b. _____

c. _____

d. _____

e. _____

f. _____

g. _____

h. _____

i. _____

j. _____

Spelling Dictation * Dictado

Pídale a alguien que le dicte las palabras de la página 92. Después de escribirlas, LÉALAS y revise la ortografía. Corrija las palabras que estén equivocadas.

Fill in the Blank * Llene el Espacio

Llene cada espacio con una palabra de la lista de palabras. Use cada palabra solamente una vez. Algunas oraciones tienen dibujos al final para ayudarle.

1. Sam is not yet _____ with lunch.

2. They _____ the big home on the hill.

3. There is a crack in the _____ .

4. _____ day he goes to his shop.

5. The boy said, "Do not _____ on me!"

6. We will _____ the bus to the camp.

7. Tom says the bus is too _____ .

8. The plants will _____ tall in the sun.

9. The rent for the car is very _____ .

10. In ten days, the plant has _____ tall.

11. The _____ cat lives in the barn.

12. Please _____ me where your dress is torn.

13. At noon my _____ is short.

14. The _____ is deep at the farm.

<u>S</u> Can Sound Like <u>Z</u>
La letra <u>s</u> puede sonar como la letra <u>z</u>

A menudo una <u>s</u> sonará como una <u>z</u>. Lea cada palabra y luego escriba el sonido de la <u>s</u> (/s/ o /z/). La primera palabra ya se ha indicado.

Word	Sound for <u>S</u>	Word	Sound for <u>S</u>
1. nose	/z/	6. brass	
2. please		7. hose	
3. rose		8. floss	
4. miss		9. goes	
5. does		10. says	

Spelling Demons * Demonios de la ortografía

Las siguientes palabras que se usan con frecuencia a menudo se escriben con mala ortografía.

would	should	could
two	twelve	twenty

Escriba una oración con cada de las palabras anteriores.

11. _____

12. _____

13. _____

14. _____

15. _____

16. _____

WordSearch * Busca Palabras

Encuentra las palabras de la Lección 15 en el busca palabras. Marca las respuestas. Las palabras pueden estar escritas en forma normal, al revés o diagonalmente.

			low
show	blow	snow	yellow
grow	own	grown	follow
every	done		

d	o	n	w	o	r	g	b	f
w	o	w	w	p	p	l	t	w
x	o	n	n	v	o	w	o	t
w	s	l	e	w	o	r	b	y
o	n	s	l	d	g	v	i	r
d	o	s	a	o	s	i	q	e
n	w	h	w	i	f	h	s	v
i	s	o	w	o	l	s	o	e
w	l	y	e	l	l	o	w	w

Answer Key * Las Respuestas

Sentences * Oraciones (page 88)

a. 5
b. 3
c. 9
d. 1
e. 4

f. 7
g. 10
h. 6
i. 8
j. 2

Spelling Dictation * Dictado (page 88)

cling, spin, spine, which, food, limp, cart, grow, one, went, hoot, hand, slow, smile, blank; Stamp the note and send it. Can Sam bake a cake?

Fill in the Blank * Llene el Espacio (page 89)

1. done
2. own
3. window
4. Every
5. blow
6. follow
7. slow

8. grow
9. low
10. grown
11. yellow
12. show
13. shadow
14. snow

<u>S</u> Can Sound Like <u>Z</u> & Spelling Demons * La letra <u>s</u> puede sonar como la letra <u>z</u> y Demonios de la ortografía (page 90)

1. z	6. s
2. z	7. z
3. z	8. s
4. s	9. z
5. z	10. z

11. – 16. Answers may vary. Las respuestas pueden variar.

WordSearch * Busca Palabras (page 91)

Reading and Spelling Check #3
Verificación de lectura y escritura #3

Haga que alguien le dicte las siguientes palabras, leyéndolas por columnas. Escriba las palabras. Cuando haya terminado de escribirlas, léalas. Al pie de esta página, escriba tres veces las palabras que escribió mal. Busque en un diccionario todas las palabras cuyo significado no conozca.

nest	lend	spent	damp
make	file	note	gone
lift	risk	done	bloom
snow	tooth	show	window
pluck	stock	broom	cart

Lesson 16 * Lección 16

Word List * Lista de palabras

El equipo de vocales <u>ai</u> crea un sonido de /a/ como en *rain*. Regla: el sonido largo de <u>a</u> generalmente se escribe como <u>ai</u> antes de una <u>n</u> o una <u>l</u>.

Inglés	Español
1. rain	lluvia
2. train	tren
3. chain	cadena
4. jail	cárcel
5. paint	pintura
6. brain	cerebro
7. stain	mancha
8. snail	caracol
9. tail	cola
10. air	aire
11. chair	silla
12. fair	feria
13. about	acerca de
14. didn't	verbo auxiliar para formar el negativo

rain

train

chain

jail

paint

brain

stain

snail

tail

chair

fair

Sentences * Oraciones

Lea las oraciones. Después escriba el número de la oración
debajo del dibujo correcto.

1. The slow snail left a trail of slime.

2. Meg will paint the shed red.

3. The dog's tail is short.

4. The long train had many boxcars.

5. The man was in jail for three days.

6. My yellow dress has a big stain.

7. The kids like to play in the rain.

8. We had fun at the fair.

9. Lock your bike with a chain.

10. Think with your brain.

Dibujos

a. _____   b. _____

c. _____

d. _____   e. _____

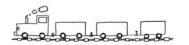

g. _____   h. _____   i. _____   j. _____

Spelling Dictation * Dictado

Pídale a alguien que le dicte las palabras de la página 99. Después de
escribirlas, LÉALAS y revise la ortografía. Corrija las palabras que estén
equivocadas.

Fill in the Blank * Llene el Espacio

Llene cada espacio con una palabra de la lista de palabras. Use cada palabra solamente una vez. Algunas oraciones tienen dibujos al final para ayudarle.

1. They ate hot dogs at the _____ .

2. The _____ smells fresh.

3. You can sit in the green _____ .

4. He wants to _____ the slide red.

5. Do not get wet in the _____ .

6. The big dog is on a long _____ .

7. The show is _____ two dogs and a cat.

8. The cat's _____ is black and yellow.

9. Use your _____ to do the test.

10. We will stand here and wait for the _____ .

11. There were four men in the _____ cell.

12. He _____ see the snake in the grass.

13. Do not smash the _____ .

14. Hide the _____ with the black paint.

96

More Practice with Homophones and Writing Sentences
Más práctica con palabras homófonas y oraciones escritas

Los homófonos suenan de manera similar, pero se escriben de manera diferente y tienen diferentes significados. Lea los homófonos a continuación y luego escriba una oración con cada homófono.

sale (venta)	sail (vela)	tail (cola)	tale (cuento)
pale (pálido)	pail (cubeta)	mail (correo)	male (varón)
pain (dolor)	pane (vidrio)	made (hecho)	maid (camarera)

1. _____

2. _____

3. _____

4. _____

5. _____

6. _____

7. _____

8. _____

9. _____

10. _____

11. _____

12. _____

WordSearch * Busca Palabras

Encuentra las palabras de la Lección 16 en el busca palabras. Marca las respuestas. Las palabras pueden estar escritas en forma normal, al revés o diagonalmente.

			air
about			

z	u	a	r	b	g	r	s	p
s	i	i	r	w	r	a	t	a
r	a	a	c	q	e	i	a	i
f	i	t	c	a	t	n	i	n
n	m	k	u	h	l	j	n	t
t	a	i	l	o	a	i	o	n
t	r	a	i	n	b	i	a	g
b	l	i	a	n	s	a	n	j
m	a	f	r	r	i	a	h	c

Answer Key * Las Respuestas

Sentences * Oraciones (page 95)

a.	5	f.	4
b.	3	g.	2
c.	8	h.	7
d.	1	i.	9
e.	10	j.	6

Spelling Dictation * Dictado (page 95)

hang, dim, dime, whale, mail, troop, frisk, hard, flow, who, band, sail, sheep, soft, blow; The cat will hunt for the mouse. Send a card to Pam.

Fill in the Blank * Llene el Espacio (page 96)

1.	fair	8.	tail
2.	air	9.	brain
3.	chair	10.	train
4.	paint	11.	jail
5.	rain	12.	didn't
6.	chain	13.	snail
7.	about	14.	stain

More Practice with Homophones and Writing Sentences * Más práctica con palabras homófonas y oraciones escritas (page 97)
1. – 12. Answers will vary. Las respuestas pueden variar.

WordSearch * Busca Palabras (page 98)

z	u	a	r	b	g	r	s	p
s	i	i	r	w	r	a	t	a
r	a	a	c	q	e	i	a	i
f	i	t	c	a	t	n	i	n
n	m	k	u	h	l	j	n	t
t	a	i	l	o	a	i	o	n
t	r	a	i	n	b	i	a	g
b	l	i	a	n	s	a	n	j
m	a	f	r	r	i	a	h	c

Lesson 17 * Lección 17

Word List * Lista de palabras

Las primeras doce palabras son palabras compuestas. Las palabras compuestas consisten de dos palabras pequeñas que forman una palabra más grande.

Inglés	Español
1. sunshine	sol
2. popcorn	palomitas de maíz
3. suntan	bronceado
4. paycheck	cheque de pago
5. hillside	ladera
6. classmate	compañero de clases
7. bedroom	recámara
8. catfish	bagre
9. pancake	panqueque
10. bathtub	tina de baño
11. rosebud	botón de rosa
12. cupcake	bizcochito
13. won	ganó
14. through	a través

sunshine

popcorn

paycheck

hillside

bedroom

catfish

pancake

bathtub

rosebud

cupcake

100

Sentences * Oraciones

Lea las oraciones. Después escriba el número de la oración debajo del dibujo correcto.

1. The sunshine will make the plums ripe.

Dibujos

2. I will use my paycheck to buy the drill.

3. There is snow on the hillside.

4. He won a toy at the fair.

a. _____   b. _____

5. There are raindrops on the rosebud.

6. The green chair is in the bedroom.

c. _____

7. We will have popcorn for a snack.

8. There is hot water in the bathtub.

9. Meg has a dark suntan.

e. _____

10. We made cupcakes for lunch.

d. _____

f. _____   g. _____

h. _____   i. _____

j. _____

Spelling Dictation * Dictado

Pídale a alguien que le dicte las palabras de la página 105. Después de escribirlas, LÉALAS y revise la ortografía. Corrija las palabras que estén equivocadas.

Fill in the Blank * Llene el Espacio

Llene cada espacio con una palabra de la lista de palabras. Use cada palabra solamente una vez. Algunas oraciones tienen dibujos al final para ayudarle.

1. They plan to paint the _____ green.

2. Whose _____ has been lost?

3. His _____ put on a red wig.

4. Do not pick the pink _____ .

5. Our four friends will sit in the _____ .

6. The ball went _____ the window.

7. Do you want a _____ with your snack?

8. Please put cool water in the _____ .

9. He and his friends _____ the baseball game.

10. Meg ate one _____ and three eggs.

11. Would you like _____ with your coke?

12. Where did you get your dark _____ ?

13. He ate _____ , chips and plums for lunch.

14. Their home is on the steep _____ .

Ending /k/ Sound * Sonido de /k/ al final

Muchas palabras en inglés terminan con el sonido /k/. Si el sonido /k/ sigue a un sonido de vocal corta, el sonido /k/ se escribe <u>ck</u>. De otra manera, /k/ se escribe <u>k</u>.

Termine cada palabra con <u>k</u> o <u>ck</u>. Después escriba la palabra completa.

1. lu_____ _____	14. for_____ _____
2. sna_____ _____	15. pa_____ _____
3. ta_____ _____	16. so_____ _____
4. sun_____ _____	17. shar_____ _____
5. sti_____ _____	18. thin_____ _____
6. sil_____ _____	19. chun_____ _____
7. bla_____ _____	20. pin_____ _____
8. du_____ _____	21. ro_____ _____
9. blin_____ _____	22. par_____ _____
10. sha_____ _____	23. tri_____ _____
11. trun_____ _____	24. drin_____ _____
12. dar_____ _____	25. ba_____ _____
13. por_____ _____	26. than_____ _____

WordSearch * Busca Palabras

Encuentra las palabras de la Lección 17 en el busca palabras. Marca las respuestas. Las palabras pueden estar escritas en forma normal, al revés o diagonalmente.

n	w	c	d	m	o	o	r	d	e	b
f	n	o	l	e	k	a	c	p	u	c
b	r	e	n	a	t	p	h	w	c	s
u	o	x	z	r	s	i	k	j	e	u
t	c	g	l	a	l	s	y	w	q	n
h	p	z	a	l	h	u	m	p	f	t
t	o	s	s	o	g	a	l	a	o	a
a	p	i	t	b	f	d	p	n	t	n
b	d	d	e	k	a	c	n	a	p	e
e	o	s	u	n	s	h	i	n	e	i
g	p	a	y	c	h	e	c	k	c	f

Answer Key * Las Respuestas

Sentences * Oraciones (page 101)

a. 7

b. 9

c. 2

d. 5

e. 6

f. 10

g. 8

h. 1

i. 3

j. 4

Spelling Dictation * Dictado (page 101)

bang, fine, rich, baseball, mail, boost, camp, bow, bend, catfish, done, tail,
cake, grow, hope; The small yellow ball is gone. Please paint the chair red.

Fill in the Blank * Llene el Espacio (page 102)

1. bedroom

2. paycheck

3. classmate

4. rosebud

5. sunshine

6. through

7. cupcake

8. bathtub

9. won

10. pancake

11. popcorn

12. suntan

13. catfish

14. hillside

Ending /k/ Sound * Sonido de /k/ al final (page 103)

1. ck luck	8. ck duck	15. ck pack	22. k park
2. ck snack	9. k blink	16. ck sock	23. ck trick
3. ck tack	10. ck shack	17. k shark	24. k drink
4. k sunk	11. k trunk	18. k think	25. ck back
5. ck stick	12. k dark	19. k chunk	26. k thank
6. k silk	13. k pork	20. k pink	
7. ck black	14. k fork	21. ck rock	

WordSearch * Busca Palabras (page 104)

Lesson 18 * Lección 18

Word List * Lista de palabras

Las primeras doce palabras terminan en mezclas. Estas mezclas son los últimos dos sonidos consonantes en cada palabra.

Inglés	Español
1. melt	derretir
2. belt	cinturón
3. felt	sintió
4. elk	alce
5. milk	leche
6. silk	seda
7. bulk	en volumen
8. crisp	crujiente
9. clasp	broche
10. grasp	agarrar
11. act	actuar
12. fact	hecho
13. know	saber
14. knew	supo

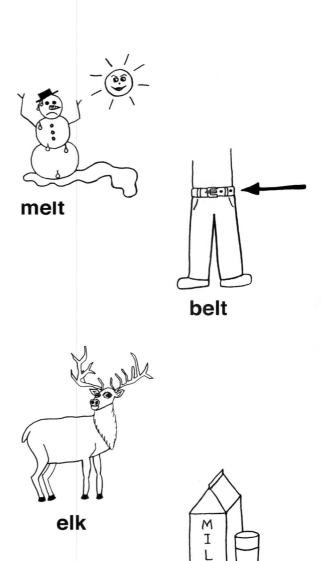

melt

belt

elk

milk

Sentences * Oraciones

Lea las oraciones. Después escriba el número de la oración debajo del dibujo correcto.

1. The boy drank a tall glass of milk.

2. Mom buys food in bulk.

3. Meg's dress is made of silk.

4. The snowman will melt in the sun.

5. Your belt is on your pants.

6. The chips are crisp and sweet.

7. Please fasten the clasp on my dress.

8. She can act with a mask.

9. The cloth felt soft.

10. When he falls, he will grasp the branch.

Dibujos

a. _____

b. _____

c. _____

e. _____

d. _____

f. _____

g. _____

h. _____

i. _____

j. _____

Spelling Dictation * Dictado

Pídale a alguien que le dicte las palabras de la página 111. Después de escribirlas, LÉALAS y revise la ortografía. Corrija las palabras que estén equivocadas.

Fill in the Blank * Llene el Espacio

Llene cada espacio con una palabra de la lista de palabras. Use cada palabra solamente una vez. Algunas oraciones tienen dibujos al final para ayudarle.

1. The _____ hid in the shadow of the tree.

2. Meg _____ how to do the math.

3. I do not want the snow to _____ .

4. Dad will buy the milk in _____ .

5. We _____ which way to go.

6. Please do not _____ like a fool.

7. Where is the pink _____ pillow?

8. Who knows this _____ about rosebuds?

9. He had _____ and a cupcake for a snack.

10. Please _____ my arm when we cross the street.

11. Sam_____ too ill to go to the farm.

12. The air is _____ and fresh today.

13. Please shut the _____ on the small silk box.

14. My black _____ is too small.

Adding ed * Adición de ed

El sufijo ed se añade a los verbos para indicar el tiempo pasado. Puede pronunciarse fonéticamente de tres maneras: /t/, /d/ y /ed/. Por ejemplo, *parkt* se escribe *parked*; *showd* se escribe *showed*; y *huntid* se escribe *hunted*.

Añada ed a los siguientes verbos y luego escriba cada verbo en la oración correcta.

grasp	wait
paint	want
show	park
cheer	crack
snow	drill

1. It _____ for three days.

2. Tom _____ a hole in the wall.

3. The small boy _____ the frog to his dad.

4. The boy _____ the red bat.

5. She _____ at the window for her friend.

6. Sam _____ to play chess with his dad.

7. The egg _____ in the sun.

8. Dad _____ at the game.

9. The man _____ his car on the grass.

10. Mom _____ the walls in the bedroom yellow.

WordSearch * Busca Palabras

Encuentra las palabras de la Lección 18 en el busca palabras. Marca las respuestas. Las palabras pueden estar escritas en forma normal, al revés o diagonalmente.

		felt	bulk
crisp	clasp	grasp	act
fact	know	knew	

k	p	f	h	c	q	r	b
n	i	s	l	f	e	l	t
o	h	a	i	e	g	s	x
w	s	a	g	r	l	s	t
p	c	o	n	j	c	k	c
t	b	u	l	k	b	h	a
g	r	a	s	p	k	u	f
k	n	e	w	t	l	e	b

Answer Key * Las Respuestas

Sentences * Oraciones (page 107)

a. 6
b. 4
c. 7
d. 9
e. 10

f. 8
g. 1
h. 5
i. 2
j. 3

Spelling Dictation * Dicatado (page 107)

lung, lime, when, snowman, train, cool, mask, low, tent, does, brain, want, bake, grow, rode; I don't know where the boys went. Wait for me by the snowman.

Fill in the Blank * Llene el Espacio (page 108)

1. elk
2. knew
3. melt
4. bulk
5. know
6. act
7. silk

8. fact
9. milk
10. grasp
11. felt
12. crisp
13. clasp
14. belt

Adding ed * Adición de ed (page 109)

1.	snowed	6.	wanted
2.	drilled	7.	cracked
3.	showed	8.	cheered
4.	grasped	9.	parked
5.	waited	10.	painted

WordSearch * Busca Palabras (page 110)

Lesson 19 * Lección 19

Word List * Lista de palabras

Las primeras doce palabras tienen el sonido /ow/ como en *cow*. Éste es el segundo sonido de /ow/. El otro sonido de <u>ow</u> es el de una /o/ larga, como en *show*.

Inglés	Español
1. cow	vaca
2. now	ahora
3. how	cómo
4. owl	búho
5. frown	ceño fruncido
6. brown	marrón
7. clown	payaso
8. town	pueblo
9. crown	corona
10. bow	reverencia
11. down	abajo
12. growl	gruñir
13. saw	vio
14. again	otra vez

cow

owl

frown

clown

crown

bow

growl

Sentences * Oraciones

Lea las oraciones. Después escriba el número de la oración debajo del dibujo correcto.

1. The man has a frown on his face.

2. The clown has a small brown crown.

3. Last week Meg got a free pup.

4. Now you may bow to the queen.

5. The cow gives us milk.

6. There is a brown owl in the tree.

7. He went to town to buy a bathtub.

8. I saw a brown belt on the rug.

9. He went down the hill on the trail.

10. The dog will growl if you get too close.

Dibujos

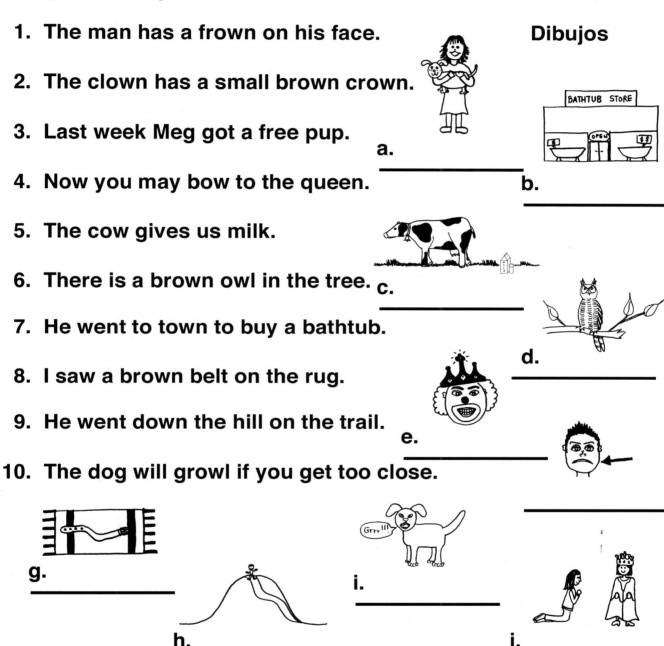

a. _____

b. _____

c. _____

d. _____

e. _____

g. _____

h. _____

i. _____

j. _____

Spelling Dictation * Dicatado

Pídale a alguien que le dicte las palabras de la página 117. Después de escribirlas, LÉALAS y revise la ortografía. Corrija las palabras que estén equivocadas.

Fill in the Blank * Llene el Espacio

Llene cada espacio con una palabra de la lista de palabras. Use cada palabra solamente una vez. Algunas oraciones tienen dibujos al final para ayudarle.

1. The dog will _____ if you take his food.

2. _____ is your mom?

3. The milk we drank is from the brown _____ .

4. Please put the vase _____ .

5. The clown had a big red _____ on his face.

6. I _____ your dad at the store.

7. The brown _____ hoots when it's dark.

8. Please show me _____ how to do the math.

9. Take a _____ when you're done.

10. _____ is the time to brush your teeth.

11. The queen's _____ is yellow, red and green.

12. The _____ chair is torn.

13. Let's meet in _____ for lunch.

14. The _____ ate hot dogs and popcorn.

114

Adding ed * Adición de ed

El sufijo ed se añade a los verbos para indicar el tiempo pasado. Puede pronunciarse fonéticamente de tres maneras: /t/, /d/ y /ed/. Por ejemplo, *parkt* se escribe *parked*; *showd* se escribe *showed*; y *huntid* se escribe *hunted*.

Añada ed a los siguientes verbos y luego escriba cada verbo en la oración correcta.

train	pump
camp	lift
growl	rent
frown	start
ask	call

1. Sam _____ his friend at the farm.

2. The game _____ at two.

3. The dog _____ at the small boy.

4. Meg _____ a car for the trip.

5. He _____ his dog to sit on the rug.

6. Tom _____ his dad if he could go to the zoo.

7. Ed _____ the sheep into the truck.

8. We _____ at the park with our tents.

9. Pam _____ gas into the truck's tank.

10. Dad _____ at the spilt milk.

WordSearch * Busca Palabras

Encuentra las palabras de la Lección 19 en el busca palabras. Marca las respuestas. Las palabras pueden estar escritas en forma normal, al revés o diagonalmente.

	now	how	brown
town	down	saw	again

c	r	o	w	n	d	w	o
d	o	w	n	n	o	w	z
n	x	n	w	b	l	w	m
l	s	o	i	c	w	r	h
n	r	h	s	a	o	o	h
b	o	p	b	a	g	w	n
w	t	o	w	n	w	a	t
u	i	q	n	w	o	l	c

Answer Key * Las Respuestas

Sentences * Oraciones (page 113)

a. 3
b. 7
c. 5
d. 6
e. 2

f. 1
g. 8
h. 9
i. 10
j. 4

Spelling Dictation * Dictado (page 113)

mine, spoon, white, wood, think, milk, hand, there, down, jail, crime, book, flow, snowman, thing; Does Meg like catfish? Did you forget the cupcakes?

Fill in the Blank * Llene el Espacio (page 114)

1. growl
2. How
3. cow
4. down
5. frown
6. saw
7. owl

8. again
9. bow
10. Now
11. crown
12. brown
13. town
14. clown

Adding ed * Adición de ed (page 115)

1. called	6. asked
2. started	7. lifted
3. growled	8. camped
4. rented	9. pumped
5. trained	10. frowned

WordSearch * Busca Palabras (page 116)

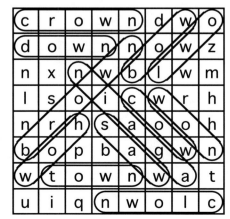

Lesson 20 * Lección 20

Word List * Lista de palabras

Las primeras doce palabras tienen el sonido /oo/ como en *good*. El otro sonido de <u>oo</u> es /oo/ como en *food*.

Inglés	Español
1. good	bueno
2. book	libro
3. look	mirar
4. cook	cocinero/cocinar
5. foot	pie
6. took	llevó
7. wood	madera
8. shook	sacudió
9. hook	gancho
10. hood	capucha
11. stood	permaneció
12. wool	lana
13. should	debería
14. could	podría

book

cook   foot

wood

hook

hood

Sentences * Oraciones

Lea las oraciones. Después escriba el número de la oración debajo del dibujo correcto.

1. The cook will fry the eggs.

Dibujos

2. His left foot has a big cut.

3. Look at all the snow on your car!

4. He has a wool hood to keep him warm.

a.
_____

b.
_____

5. She stood in the rain to wait for the bus.

6. Those clams are really good.

7. Sam hung his hat on the hook.

c.
_____

d.
_____

8. Pam will put some wood on the fire.

9. The man took his paycheck to the bank.

10. The book is about a cow and an owl.

e.
_____

f.
_____

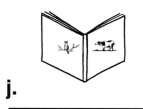

g.
_____

h.
_____

i.
_____

j.
_____

Spelling Dictation * Dictado

Pídale a alguien que le dicte las palabras de la página 123. Después de escribirlas, LÉALAS y revise la ortografía. Corrija las palabras que estén equivocadas.

Fill in the Blank * Llene el Espacio

Llene cada espacio con una palabra de la lista de palabras. Use cada palabra solamente una vez. Algunas oraciones tienen dibujos al final para ayudarle.

1. Please put on your _____ to keep warm.

2. You _____ brush your teeth three times a day.

3. Ted wants to _____ a big fish.

4. He _____ on the hillside to look for the lost sheep.

5. Their home is made of _____ .

6. The small boy _____ too many chips.

7. Your _____ about cats is on the top shelf.

8. Is that a _____ book?

9. We _____ only see one owl in the tree.

10. Dad will _____ ham and eggs for lunch.

11. He _____ the dust off his pants.

12. Bob's _____ pants have a hole at the knee.

13. Tom's _____ is too big for that sock.

14. Please help me _____ for my cane.

120

English Words With More Than One Meaning
Palabras en inglés con más de un significado

Muchas palabras en inglés tienen más de un significado. Use la palabra correcta en cada una de las oraciones.

Bat murciélago o bate de béisbol	**Fair** juego justo o ir a la feria
Train tren o entrenar al perro	**Left** lado izquierdo o dejó atrás
Show mostrar o espectáculo	**Saw** vio o sierra
Back espalda o regreso	**Shed** cabaña o mudar pelo

1. The _____ passes by the town at four.

2. There is a big red bug on your _____ .

3. The _____ hangs by its feet when it sleeps in a cave.

4. The snake will _____ its skin.

5. Sam will _____ his dog to stand on two feet.

6. I _____ the brown cow in the barn.

7. I will bring my _____ and ball to the game.

8. Please _____ me the five pups.

9. We _____ our books in class.

10. Please give me _____ my books.

11. The _____ starts at nine.

12. He won a big stuffed dog at the _____ .

13. Your _____ is in the tool shed.

14. There is a rash on my _____ arm.

15. That boy does not play _____ .

16. The cats live in the _____ .

WordSearch * Busca Palabras

Encuentra las palabras de la Lección 20 en el busca palabras. Marca las respuestas. Las palabras pueden estar escritas en forma normal, al revés o diagonalmente.

		wool	**good**
look	**took**	**shook**	**stood**
should	**could**		

n	k	v	h	g	k	k	k	k
o	u	o	o	o	s	o	o	s
v	o	o	o	h	o	o	k	t
k	d	c	o	h	t	a	a	o
u	c	u	s	h	k	b	y	o
s	l	o	k	f	o	o	k	d
d	m	c	u	o	o	o	o	r
w	o	o	l	l	o	o	d	l
n	d	o	o	w	d	b	t	g

Answer Key * Las Respuestas

Sentences * Oraciones (page 119)

a. 8

b. 3

c. 6

d. 1

e. 7

f. 9

g. 2

h. 5

i. 4

j. 10

Spelling Dictation * Dictado (page 119)

vote, stood, when, shook, faint, dust, left, where, brown, drain, bake, shadow, hillside, clown, hung; We went for a ride on the train. The wet dog ran from the pond.

Fill in the Blank * Llene el Espacio (page 120)

1. hood
2. should
3. hook
4. stood
5. wood
6. took
7. book

8. good
9. could
10. cook
11. shook
12. wool
13. foot
14. look

Words With More Than One Meaning * Palabras en inglés con más de un significado (page 121)

1.	train	9.	left
2.	back	10.	back
3.	bat	11.	show
4.	shed	12.	fair
5.	train	13.	saw
6.	saw	14.	left
7.	bat	15.	fair
8.	show	16.	shed

WordSearch * Busca Palabras (page 122)

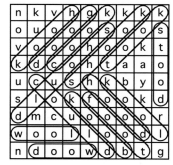

Reading and Spelling Check #4
Verificación de lectura y escritura #4

Haga que alguien le dicte las siguientes palabras, leyéndolas por columnas. Escriba las palabras. Cuando haya terminado de escribirlas, léalas. Al pie de esta página, escriba tres veces las palabras que escribió mal. Busque en un diccionario todas las palabras cuyo significado no conozca.

slide	blow	won	feet
paint	again	trade	glow
stand	must	trail	they
smooth	pink	gift	pump
went	mall	mule	book

English Translation of Spanish Directions

Lesson 1

Page 1: When y comes at the end of a short word, it has the sound of long /i/ as in *by*.

Page 2: Read the sentences. Then put the number of the sentence under the correct picture. **Spelling Dictation** Have someone dictate the words on page 6 to you. After you have written the words READ THE WORDS and check to make sure they are spelled correctly. Correct any words that are misspelled.

Page 3: Fill in each blank with a word from the Word List. Use each word once. Some sentences have pictures at the end to help you.

Page 4: When adding an s to words that end in y, you will need to drop the y and add ies except when the y is preceded by a vowel as in *boy/boys*. Use the words at the right to fill in the blanks. Drop the y and add ies when necessary.

Page 5: Find the words from Lesson 1 in the WordSearch. Circle the words. The words can be written across, in reverse, or diagonal.

Lesson 2

Page 7: The e or o at the end of short words will usually be long vowel sounds. Exceptions are to and do.

Page 8: Read the sentences. Then put the number of the sentence under the correct picture. **Spelling Dictation** Have someone dictate the words on page 12 to you. After you have written the words READ THE WORDS and check to make sure they are spelled correctly. Correct any words that are misspelled.

Page 9: Fill in each blank with a word from the Word List. Use each word once. Some sentences have pictures at the end to help you.

Page 10: The letter v is never used at the end of a word. In words ending with a v sound such as have, give, live, the marker e is placed at the end of the word so it does not violate the "v" rule. The vowel sound can be either long or short. Use the words above in the sentences below. Use each word once. **Rhyming Words.** Rhyming words are words that begin differently but end with the same vowel and ending sounds. For example, *red, bed*, and *said* are rhyming words. They do not need to be spelled the same, but they do need to end with the same vowel and ending sounds. Use the words at the right to match rhyming words.

Page 11: Find the words from Lesson 2 in the WordSearch. Circle the words. The words can be written across, in reverse, or diagonal.

Lesson 3

Page 13: Blend the consonant and vowel sounds to read and spell the words. <u>Ch</u> says <u>/ch/</u> as in <u>chip</u>.

Page 14: Read the sentences. Then put the number of the sentence under the correct picture. **Spelling Dictation** Have someone dictate the words on page 18 to you. After you have written the words READ THE WORDS and check to make sure they are spelled correctly. Correct any words that are misspelled.

Page 15: Fill in each blank with a word from the Word List. Use each word once. Some sentences have pictures at the end to help you.

Page 16: The following frequently used words are often misspelled. Use the words above in the sentences below. Use each word once. **Rhyming Words.** Rhyming words are words that begin differently but end with the same vowel and ending sounds. For example, *red*, *bed*, and *said* are rhyming words. They do not need to be spelled the same, but they do need to end with the same vowel and ending sounds. If the two words rhyme, write "yes." If not, write "no."

Page 17: Find the words from Lesson 3 in the WordSearch. Circle the words. The words can be written across, in reverse, or diagonal.

Lesson 4

Page 19: Blend the consonant and vowel sounds to read and spell the words. <u>Or</u> says /or/ as in *corn*.

Page 20: Read the sentences. Then put the number of the sentence under the correct picture. **Spelling Dictation** Have someone dictate the words on page 24 to you. After you have written the words READ THE WORDS and check to make sure they are spelled correctly. Correct any words that are misspelled.

Page 21: Fill in each blank with a word from the Word List. Use each word once. Some sentences have pictures at the end to help you.

Page 22: Use the following verbs in the sentences below. Use each verb once. **Rhyming Words**. Rhyming words are words that begin differently but end with the same vowel and ending sounds. For example, *red*, *bed*, and *said* are rhyming words. They do not need to be spelled the same, but they do need to end with the same vowel and ending sounds. Use the words at the right to match rhyming words.

Page 23: Find the words from Lesson 4 in the WordSearch. Circle the words. The words can be written across, in reverse, or diagonal.

Lesson 5

Page 25: Blend the sounds to read and spell the words. <u>All</u> says /all/ as in *ball*.

Page 26: Read the sentences. Then put the number of the sentence under the correct picture. **Spelling Dictation** Have someone dictate the words on page 30 to you. After you have written the words READ THE WORDS and check to make sure they are spelled correctly. Correct any words that are misspelled.

Page 27: Fill in each blank with a word from the Word List. Use each word once. Some sentences have pictures at the end to help you.

Page 28: The following frequently used words are often misspelled. Use the words above in the sentences below. Use each word once. **Rhyming Words.** Rhyming words are words that begin differently but end with the same vowel and ending sounds. For example, *red*, *bed*, and *said* are rhyming words. They do not need to be spelled the same, but they do need to end with the same vowel and ending sounds. If the two words rhyme, write "yes." If not, write "no."

Page 29: Find the words from Lesson 5 in the WordSearch. Circle the words. The words can be written across, in reverse, or diagonal.

Reading and Spelling Check #1

Page 31: Have someone dictate the following words to you, reading down the columns. Write the words. When you have finished writing the words, read the words. At the bottom of this page, write any misspelled words three times. Look up the words in a dictionary if you do not know their meanings.

Lesson 6

Page 32: Blend the consonant and vowel sounds to read and spell the words. <u>Th</u> has two sounds, one voiced and one unvoiced. The <u>th</u> says /th/ as in *that* or *thin*.

Page 33: Read the sentences. Then put the number of the sentence under the correct picture. **Spelling Dictation** Have someone dictate the words on page 37 to you. After you have written the words READ THE WORDS and check to make sure they are spelled correctly. Correct any words that are misspelled.

Page 34: Fill in each blank with a word from the Word List. Use each word once. Some sentences have pictures at the end to help you.

Page 35: To show ownership you need to add an apostrophe <u>s</u> ('s) to the noun. Use the following words to fill in the sentences. Remember to add an apostrophe <u>s</u> ('s) to show ownership. Use the words above in the sentences below. Use each word once. **Rhyming**

Words. Rhyming words are words that begin differently but end with the same vowel and ending sounds. For example, *red*, *bed*, and *said* are rhyming words. They do not need to be spelled the same, but they do need to end with the same vowel and ending sounds. Write two words that rhyme with the word in the first column.

Page 36: Find the words from Lesson 6 in the WordSearch. Circle the words. The words can be written across, in reverse, or diagonal.

Lesson 7

Page 38: Blend the consonant and vowel sounds to read and spell the words. The letters ing say /ing/ as in *sing*, the letters ang say /ang/ as in *sang*, the letters ong say /ong/ as in *song*, and the letters ung say /ung/ as in *sung*.

Page 39: Read the sentences. Then put the number of the sentence under the correct picture. **Spelling Dictation** Have someone dictate the words on page 43 to you. After you have written the words READ THE WORDS and check to make sure they are spelled correctly. Correct any words that are misspelled.

Page 40: Fill in each blank with a word from the Word List. Use each word once. Some sentences have pictures at the end to help you.

Page 41: The following frequently used words are often misspelled. Use the words above in the sentences below. Use each word once. **Rhyming Words.** Rhyming words are words that begin differently but end with the same vowel and ending sounds. For example, *red*, *bed*, and *said* are rhyming words. They do not need to be spelled the same, but they do need to end with the same vowel and ending sounds. Write two words that rhyme with the first word in each row.

Page 42: Find the words from Lesson 7 in the WordSearch. Circle the words. The words can be written across, in reverse, or diagonal.

Lesson 8

Page 44: Blend the consonant and vowel sounds to read and spell the words. The letters oy are pronounced /oy/ as in *boy*. Rule: the letters oy are generally found at the end of a word. The letters ar are pronounced /ar/ as in *car*.

Page 45: Read the sentences. Then put the number of the sentence under the correct picture. **Spelling Dictation** Have someone dictate the words on page 49 to you. After you have written the words READ THE WORDS and check to make sure they are spelled correctly. Correct any words that are misspelled.

Page 46: Fill in each blank with a word from the Word List. Use each word once. Some sentences have pictures at the end to help you.

Page 47: Drop the final sound in each word to make a new word. Drop the last letter in each word to make a new word.

Page 48: Find the words from Lesson 8 in the WordSearch. Circle the words. The words can be written across, in reverse, or diagonal.

Lesson 9

Page 50: Blend the consonant and vowel sounds to read and spell the words. The <u>wh</u> says /wh/ as in *wheel*. Rule: <u>wh</u> comes at the beginning of a word. In most parts of the United States, <u>wh</u> and <u>w</u> sound the same.

Page 51: Read the sentences. Then put the number of the sentence under the correct picture. **Spelling Dictation** Have someone dictate the words on page 55 to you. After you have written the words READ THE WORDS and check to make sure they are spelled correctly. Correct any words that are misspelled.

Page 52: Fill in each blank with a word from the Word List. Use each word once. Some sentences have pictures at the end to help you.

Page 53: Write question sentences using each of the following words. **Making New Words.** Drop the first letter in the original word to make a new word. The first one has been done for you.

Page 54: Find the words from Lesson 9 in the WordSearch. Circle the words. The words can be written across, in reverse, or diagonal.

Lesson 10

Page 56: Blend the consonant and vowel sounds to read and spell the words. Rule: <u>-k</u> is the first choice for /k/ at the end of a word after a consonant, a long vowel or a double vowel. The letters <u>–ck</u> come at the end of a word after a short vowel.

Page 57: Read the sentences. Then put the number of the sentence under the correct picture. **Spelling Dictation** Have someone dictate the words on page 61 to you. After you have written the words READ THE WORDS and check to make sure they are spelled correctly. Correct any words that are misspelled.

Page 58: Fill in each blank with a word from the Word List. Use each word once. Some sentences have pictures at the end to help you.

Page 59: Use the words below to fill in the blanks. You may need to use a dictionary.

Page 60: Find the words from Lesson 10 in the WordSearch. Circle the words. The words can be written across, in reverse, or diagonal.

Reading and Spelling Check #2

Page 62: Have someone dictate the following words to you, reading down the columns. Write the words. When you have finished writing the words, read the words. At the bottom of this page, write any misspelled words three times. Look up the words in a dictionary if you not know their meanings.

Lesson 11

Page 63: Blend the consonant and vowel sounds to read and spell the words. The letters <u>oo</u> are pronounced /oo/ as in *food*. Rule: <u>oo</u> usually comes in the middle of a word.

Page 64: Read the sentences. Then put the number of the sentence under the correct picture. **Spelling Dictation** Have someone dictate the words on page 68 to you. After you have written the words READ THE WORDS and check to make sure they are spelled correctly. Correct any words that are misspelled.

Page 65: Fill in each blank with a word from the Word List. Use each word once. Some sentences have pictures at the end to help you.

Page 66: Leave out one letter in the original word to make a new word. The first one has been done for you. **Homophones** A homophone is a word that sounds like another but has a different spelling and a different meaning. The following homophones are among the most often misspelled words in the English language. Write sentences using each homophone correctly.

Page 67: Find the words from Lesson 11 in the WordSearch. Circle the words. The words can be written across, in reverse, or diagonal.

Lesson 12

Page 69: The <u>e</u> on the end of a word makes the preceding vowel say its name. This the the Vowel-Consonant-e pattern.

Page 70: Read the sentences. Then put the number of the sentence under the correct picture. **Spelling Dictation** Have someone dictate the words on page 74 to you. After you have written the words READ THE WORDS and check to make sure they are spelled correctly. Correct any words that are misspelled.

Page 71: Fill in each blank with a word from the Word List. Use each word once. Some sentences have pictures at the end to help you.

Page 72: Add a silent <u>e</u> to the end of each word to make a new word. **Writing Sentences** Write sentences using the following words. Remember each sentence begins with a capital letter and ends with one of the three punctuation marks. (. ? !)

Page 73: Find the words from Lesson 12 in the WordSearch. Circle the words. The words can be written across, in reverse, or diagonal.

Lesson 13

Page 75: The first twelve words end in blends. These blends are the last two consonant sounds in each word.

Page 76: Read the sentences. Then put the number of the sentence under the correct picture. **Spelling Dictation** Have someone dictate the words on page 80 to you. After you have written the words READ THE WORDS and check to make sure they are spelled correctly. Correct any words that are misspelled.

Page 77: Fill in each blank with a word from the Word List. Use each word once. Some sentences have pictures at the end to help you.

Page 78: Compound words contain two small words to make one word. Use the two small words to make a compound word. Write seven sentences using a different compound word in each one.

Page 79: Find the words from Lesson 13 in the WordSearch. Circle the words. The words can be written across, in reverse, or diagonal.

Lesson 14

Page 81: The first twelve words end in blends. These blends are the last two consonant sounds in each word.

Page 82: Read the sentences. Then put the number of the sentence under the correct picture. **Spelling Dictation** Have someone dictate the words on page 86 to you. After you have written the words READ THE WORDS and check to make sure they are spelled correctly. Correct any words that are misspelled.

Page 83: Fill in each blank with a word from the Word List. Use each word once. Some sentences have pictures at the end to help you.

Page 84: The following frequently used words are often misspelled. Use the words above in the sentences below. Use each word once. **Words Ending in s** Sometimes when a word ends in s, the s will sound like /z/. Tell whether each s says /s/ or /z/. The first one has been done for you.

Page 85: Find the words from Lesson 14 in the WordSearch. Circle the words. The words can be written across, in reverse, or diagonal.

Lesson 15

Page 87: The first twelve words end in <u>ow</u>. In this list, the <u>ow</u> makes the long /o/ sound as in *low*. Rule: <u>ow</u> comes at the end of a word, or it may be followed by an <u>n</u>.

Page 88: Read the sentences. Then put the number of the sentence under the correct picture. **Spelling Dictation** Have someone dictate the words on page 92 to you. After you have written the words READ THE WORDS and check to make sure they are spelled correctly. Correct any words that are misspelled.

Page 89: Fill in each blank with a word from the Word List. Use each word once. Some sentences have pictures at the end to help you.

Page 90: Often an <u>s</u> will sound like a <u>z</u>. Read each word then write the sound for <u>s</u> (/s/ or /z/). The first one has been done for you. **Spelling Demons** The following frequently used words are often misspelled. Write a sentence with each of the words above.

Page 91: Find the words from Lesson 15 in the WordSearch. Circle the words. The words can be written across, in reverse, or diagonal.

Reading and Spelling Check #3

Page 93: Have someone dictate the following words to you, reading down the columns. Write the words. When you have finished writing the words, read the words. At the bottom of this page, write any misspelled words three times. Look up the words in a dictionary if you do not know their meanings.

Lesson 16

Page 94: The vowel team <u>ai</u> makes a long /a/ sound as in *rain*. Rule: The long sound of <u>a</u> is usually spelled <u>ai</u> before <u>n</u> or <u>l</u>.

Page 95: Read the sentences. Then put the number of the sentence under the correct picture. **Spelling Dictation** Have someone dictate the words on page 99 to you. After you have written the words READ THE WORDS and check to make sure they are spelled correctly. Correct any words that are misspelled.

Page 96: Fill in each blank with a word from the Word List. Use each word once. Some sentences have pictures at the end to help you.

Page 97: Homophones sound alike, but are spelled differently and have different meanings. Read the homophones below, then write a sentence using each homophone.

Page 98: Find the words from Lesson 16 in the WordSearch. Circle the words. The words can be written across, in reverse, or diagonal.

Lesson 17

Page 100: The first twelve words are compound words. Compound words consist of two small words to make one large word.

Page 101: Read the sentences. Then put the number of the sentence under the correct picture. **Spelling Dictation** Have someone dictate the words on page 105 to you. After you have written the words READ THE WORDS and check to make sure they are spelled correctly. Correct any words that are misspelled.

Page 102: Fill in each blank with a word from the Word List. Use each word once. Some sentences have pictures at the end to help you.

Page 103: Many words in English end with the /k/ sound. If the /k/ sound immediately follows a short vowel sound, the /k/ spelling will be <u>ck</u>. Otherwise the spelling for /k/ will be <u>k</u>. Complete each word with <u>k</u> or <u>ck</u>. Then write the entire word.

Page 104: Find the words from Lesson 17 in the WordSearch. Circle the words. The words can be written across, in reverse, or diagonal.

Lesson 18

Page 106: The first twelve words end with blends. These blends are the two consonant sounds at the beginning of the words.

Page 107: Read the sentences. Then put the number of the sentence under the correct picture. **Spelling Dictation** Have someone dictate the words on page 111 to you. After you have written the words READ THE WORDS and check to make sure they are spelled correctly. Correct any words that are misspelled.

Page 108: Fill in each blank with a word from the Word List. Use each word once. Some sentences have pictures at the end to help you.

Page 109: The suffix <u>ed</u> is added to verbs to show past tense. It can be spoken phonetically in three different ways /t/, /d/, and /ed/. For example *parkt* is spelled *parked*; *showd* is spelled *showed*; and *hunted* is spelled *hunted*. Add <u>ed</u> to the following verbs then write each verb in the correct sentence.

Page 110: Find the words from Lesson 18 in the WordSearch. Circle the words. The words can be written across, in reverse, or diagonal.

Lesson 19

Page 112: The first twelve words have the /ow/ sound as in *cow*. This is the second sound for /ow/. The other sound for <u>ow</u> is long /o/ as in *show*.

Page 113: Read the sentences. Then put the number of the sentence under the correct picture. **Spelling Dictation** Have someone dictate the words on page 117 to you. After you have written the words READ THE WORDS and check to make sure they are spelled correctly. Correct any words that are misspelled.

Page 114: Fill in each blank with a word from the Word List. Use each word once. Some sentences have pictures at the end to help you.

Page 115: The suffix ed is added to verbs to show past tense. It can be spoken phonetically in three different ways /t/, /d/, and /ed/. For example *parkt* is spelled *parked*; *showd* is spelled *showed*; and *hunted* is spelled *hunted*. Add ed to the following verbs then write each verb in the correct sentence.

Page 116: Find the words from Lesson 19 in the WordSearch. Circle the words. The words can be written across, in reverse, or diagonal.

Lesson 20

Page 118: The first twelve words have the /oo/ sound as in *good*. The other sound for oo is /oo/ as in *food*.

Page 119: Read the sentences. Then put the number of the sentence under the correct picture. **Spelling Dictation** Have someone dictate the words on page 123 to you. After you have written the words READ THE WORDS and check to make sure they are spelled correctly. Correct any words that are misspelled.

Page 120: Fill in each blank with a word from the Word List. Use each word once. Some sentences have pictures at the end to help you.

Page 121: Many English words have more than one meaning. Use the correct word in each sentence.

bat (animal or baseball bat)	**fair** (play fair or go to the fair)
train (transportation or train the dog)	**left** (left hand or left behind)
show (show me or watch the show)	**saw** (to see or a tool)
back (part of the body or to return)	**shed** (small building or shed hair)

Page 122: Find the words from Lesson 20 in the WordSearch. Circle the words. The words can be written across, in reverse, or diagonal.

Reading and Spelling Check #4

Page 124: Have someone dictate the following words to you, reading down the columns. Write the words. When you have finished writing the words, read the words. At the bottom of this page, write any misspelled words three times. Look up the words in a dictionary if you not know their meanings.

Índice

Index

Books Available From **FISHER HILL**
For Ages 10-Adult

ENGLISH READING COMPREHENSION FOR THE SPANISH SPEAKER Book 1, 2, 3, 4, & 5

ENGLISH READING AND SPELLING FOR THE SPANISH SPEAKER Books 1, 2, 3, 4, 5 & 6

ENGLISH for the SPANISH SPEAKER Books 1, 2, 3, 4 & Cassettes

SPANISH made FUN and EASY Books 1 & 2

HEALTH Easy to Read

UNITED STATES OF AMERICA Stories, Maps, Activities in Spanish and English Books 1, 2, 3, & 4

English Reading Comprehension for the Spanish Speaker Books 1, 2, 3, 4, & 5 contain twenty lessons to help Spanish-speaking students improve their English reading comprehension skills. Lessons include practice with vocabulary, visualization, fluency, phonology, and comprehension. Each lesson has an answer key. These are excellent books to use after completing *English Reading and Spelling for the Spanish Speaker Books 1, 2, 3, 4, & 5*. Price is $15.95, size is 8 1/2 x11 and each book is approximately 161 pages. Book 1 ISBN 978-1-878253-37-8, Book 2 ISBN 978-1-878253-43-9, Book 3 ISBN 978-1-878253-44-6, Book 4 ISBN 978-1-878253-47-7, Book 5 ISBN 978-1-878253-48-4

English Reading and Spelling for the Spanish Speaker Books 1, 2, 3, 4, 5 & 6 contain twenty lessons to help Spanish-speaking students learn to read and spell English. The books use a systematic approach in teaching the English speech sounds and other phonological skills. They also present basic sight words that are not phonetic. The word lists are in Spanish and English and all directions are in Spanish with English translations. Each book is $14.95 and approximately 142 pages. Book size is 8 1/2 x 11. Book 1 ISBN 978-1-878253-27-9, Book 2 ISBN 978-1-878253-25-5, Book 3 ISBN 978-1-878253-26-2, Book 4 ISBN 978-1-878253-29-3, Book 5 ISBN 978-1-878253-30-9, Book 6 ISBN 978-1-878253-35-4.

ENGLISH for the SPANISH SPEAKER Books 1, 2, 3, & 4 are English as a Second Language workbooks for ages 10 - adult. Each book is divided into eight lessons and is written in Spanish and English. Each lesson includes: vocabulary, a conversation, a story, four activity pages, an answer key, two dictionaries: English-Spanish and Spanish-English, a puzzle section, and an index. Each book is $12.95 and approximately 110 pages. Book size is 8 1/2 x 11. Book 1 ISBN 978-1-878253-07-1, Book 2 ISBN 978-1-878253-16-3, Book 3 ISBN 978-1-878253-17-0, Book 4 ISBN 978-1-878253-18-7; Book 1 Cassette ISBN 978-1-878253-21-7, Book 2 Cassette ISBN 978-1-878253-32-3, Book 3 Cassette ISBN 978-1-878253-33-0, Book 4 Cassette ISBN 978-1-878253-34-7.

SPANISH made FUN and EASY Books 1 & 2 are workbooks for ages 10 - adult. Each book includes stories, games, conversations, activity pages, vocabulary lists, dictionaries, and an index. The books are for beginning Spanish students; people who want to brush up on high school Spanish; or for Spanish speakers who want to learn how to read and write Spanish. Each book is $14.95 and 134 pages. Book size is 8 1/2 x 11. Book 1 ISBN 978-1-878253-42-2, Book 2 ISBN 978-1-878253-46-0.

HEALTH Easy to Read contains 21 easy to read stories. After each story is a vocabulary page, a grammar page, and a question and answer page. The stories are about changing people's life styles to reduce their risk of poor health and premature death. Book is $13.95 and has 118 pages. Book size is 8 1/2 x 11. ISBN 978-1-878253-41-5.

United STATES of America Stories, Maps, Activities in SPANISH and ENGLISH Books 1, 2, 3, & 4 are easy to read books about the United States of America for ages 10 - adult. Each state is presented by a story, map, and activities. Each book contains information for 12 to 13 states and has an answer key and index. The states are presented in alphabetical order. Book size is 8 1/2 x 11. Each book is $14.95 and approximately 140 pages.
Book 1 ISBN 978-1-878253-49-1 Alabama through Idaho
Book 2 ISBN 978-1-878253-11-8 Illinois through Missouri
Book 3 ISBN 978-1-878253-12-5 Montana through Pennsylvania
Book 4 ISBN 978-1-878253-13-2 Rhode Island through Wyoming

Toll Free Ordering
1-800-214-8110
Monday-Friday 8am-5pm
Central Standard Time

Order by Fax
714-377-9495

Fisher Hill

5267 Warner Ave., #166
Huntington Beach, CA 92649-4079
www.Fisher-Hill.com

Order On-Line
www.Fisher-Hill.com

Questions or Concerns
714-377-9353

Purchase Order Number: _____

Bill To:
Name: _____
Address: _____
City: _____ State _____ ZIP _____
Phone: _____

Ship To: (if different than billing address)
Name: _____
Address: _____
City: _____ State _____ ZIP _____
Phone: _____

QUANTITY	ISBN	BOOK TITLE	PRICE	AMOUNT
	37-8	English Reading Comprehension for the Spanish Speaker Book 1	$15.95	
	43-9	English Reading Comprehension for the Spanish Speaker Book 2	$15.95	
	44-6	English Reading Comprehension for the Spanish Speaker Book 3	$15.95	
	47-7	English Reading Comprehension for the Spanish Speaker Book 4	$15.95	
	48-4	English Reading Comprehension for the Spanish Speaker Book 5	$15.95	
	27-9	English Reading and Spelling for the Spanish Speaker Book 1	$14.95	
	25-5	English Reading and Spelling for the Spanish Speaker Book 2	$14.95	
	26-2	English Reading and Spelling for the Spanish Speaker Book 3	$14.95	
	29-3	English Reading and Spelling for the Spanish Speaker Book 4	$14.95	
	30-9	English Reading and Spelling for the Spanish Speaker Book 5	$14.95	
	35-4	English Reading and Spelling for the Spanish Speaker Book 6	$14.95	
	07-1	English For The Spanish Speaker Book 1	$12.95	
	21-7	English For The Spanish Speaker Book 1 Cassette	$10.95	
	20-0	English For The Spanish Speaker Book 1 and Cassette	$21.95	
	16-3	English For The Spanish Speaker Book 2	$12.95	
	32-3	English For The Spanish Speaker Book 2 Cassette	$10.95	
	38-5	English For The Spanish Speaker Book 2 and Cassette	$21.95	
	17-0	English For The Spanish Speaker Book 3	$12.95	
	33-0	English For The Spanish Speaker Book 3 Cassette	$10.95	
	39-2	English For The Spanish Speaker Book 3 and Cassette	$21.95	
	18-7	English For The Spanish Speaker Book 4	$12.95	
	34-7	English For The Spanish Speaker Book 4 Cassette	$10.95	
	40-8	English For The Spanish Speaker Book 4 and Cassette	$21.95	
	41-5	HEALTH Easy to Read	$13.95	
	49-1	USA Stories, Maps, Activities in Spanish & English Book 1	$14.95	
	11-8	USA Stories, Maps, Activities in Spanish & English Book 2	$14.95	
	12-5	USA Stories, Maps, Activities in Spanish & English Book 3	$14.95	
	13-2	USA Stories, Maps, Activities in Spanish & English Book 4	$14.95	
	42-2	SPANISH made FUN & EASY Book 1	$14.95	
	46-0	SPANISH made FUN & EASY Book 2	$14.95	
	MW920-7	Diccionario Español-Inglés	$6.50	
	MW852-1	Diccionario de Sinónimos y Antónimos en Inglés	$6.50	
	MW890-3	Juego de Diccionarios	$19.50	
	MW605-3	Dictionary of Basic English	$9.95	

Credit Card Information
Card Number: _____
Expiration Date: _____
Name: _____
Address: _____
City: _____ State _____ ZIP _____
Phone: _____

TOTAL _____

Add 7.75% for shipments to California addresses. SALES TAX _____

Add 10% of TOTAL for shipping. (Minimum $4.00) SHIPPING _____

PAYMENT _____

BALANCE DUE _____